Personnel Manager's Portfolio of Model Letters

Also by the author

Human Resource Director's Handbook, Prentice-Hall, Inc., 1984

Personnel Manager's Portfolio of Model Letters

Mary F. Cook

Prentice-Hall, Inc.

Englewood Cliffs, New Jersey

Prentice-Hall International, Inc., *London*
Prentice-Hall of Australia, Pty. Ltd., *Sydney*
Prentice-Hall Canada, Inc., *Toronto*
Prentice-Hall of India Private Ltd., *New Delhi*
Prentice-Hall of Japan, Inc., *Tokyo*
Prentice-Hall of Southeast Asia Pte. Ltd., *Singapore*
Whitehall Books, Ltd., Wellington, *New Zealand*
Editora Prentice-Hall do Brasil Ltda., *Rio de Janeiro*

© 1985 *by*

PRENTICE-HALL, INC.

Englewood Cliffs, N.J.

Library of Congress Cataloging in Publication Data

Cook, Mary F.
  Personnel manager's portfolio of model letters.

  Includes index.
  1. Form letters. 2. Personnel management.
I.Title
HF5733.F6C66 1984   651.7′5   84-15065

ISBN 0-13-659251-1

Printed in the United States of America

ACKNOWLEDGMENTS

Several of my business friends and associates have contributed letters to this portfolio of model letters. They have provided specific expertise in their own areas of experience in the personnel function. The letters they have contributed are ones that address the toughest personnel issues. Regulatory compliance and personnel policy and procedural chapters are strengthened by these excellent contributions. Many thanks to the following contributors:

Barbara L. Allen
Assistant Vice President Personnel
Security Life of Denver

Richard T. Bell
Manager Employee Relations
    Administration
Rocky Mountain Energy Company
Broomfield, Colorado

E. J. Busch, Jr.
Director, Corporate Personnel
The Gates Corporation
Denver, Colorado

Raymond G. Delisle
Ihrig, Delisle & Associates
Denver, Colorado

Phyllis J. Engen
Technical Director
Corporate Human Resources
Presbyterian/St. Luke's
    Medical Center
Denver, Colorado

Carolyn L. Hayes, RN, BS
Administrator, Occupational,
    Environmental & Preventive
    Medicine
Denver Clinic
Denver, Colorado

Mary H. Henderson
Legal Assistant
Natural Resources
Union Pacific Corporation
Casper, Wyoming

Judy Leinweber
Denver, Colorado

Myrna D. Mourning
Employee Relations Consultant
United Bank of Denver
Denver, Colorado

Patty Ptacek
Manager, Corporate
    Employee Relations
Manville Corporation
Denver, Colorado

Edwin J. Quinn, Jr.
Assistant Vice President
    and Personnel Manager
United Bank of Littleton
Littleton, Colorado

Dan Schaeffer
Manager Employee Selection
    & Development
Rocky Mountain Energy Company
Broomfield, Colorado

Sherman & Howard
A Law Partnership Including
    Professional Corporations
Denver, Colorado

Marilyn Showers
Golden Hill Secretarial
Golden, Colorado

Don R. Simon
Partner
STM Associates
Salt Lake City, Utah

Myron Treber
Vice President, Human Resources
Baldwin Data Services
Denver, Colorado

How This Portfolio
Helps Personnel Managers
Meet Key Needs

Personnel Manager's Portfolio of Model Letters provides a quick, easy way to write all your personnel and human-resource-related correspondence without wasting valuable time.

In talking with other personnel professionals, I've found they agree that many personnel letters are difficult to write, especially the ones to various regulatory agencies, or to employees where tough subjects such as discipline or discharge are the issue. Most executives say that when they have written a letter that they found to be effective and worked well in a given situation, they retained a copy and added it to their personal collection of business letters for future reference. This *Portfolio* is intended to provide a broad base to serve as a handy guide to all of the various letters the personnel manager must write.

Letters included in the *Portfolio* are actual letters used in top organizations. The names have been changed to retain the privacy of individuals, but the content is actual. These letters are proven and tested for getting top results in the personnel function.

Lengthy research went into the compilation of the more than 200 personnel letters, paying particular attention to legal, organizational, and emotional issues on the subjects covered.

A key feature of the *Portfolio* is the Letter Locater Index, which speeds the location process. If you are looking for a sample letter to go to a regulatory executive, turn to the regulatory compliance section of the Index and review the list of letters included. This Index, arranged according to the individuals or groups to whom your letters are addressed, also highlights letters that go to vendors, managers, employees, local officials, outside organizations and universities, and executives. The Table of Contents lists all of the letters by major personnel responsibility, such as recruiting, compensation, benefits, regulatory compliance, development programs, community relations, personnel procedures and policies, health and safety, and others.

Tough issues such as discipline and discharge, charges of sexual harassment, and sex and age discrimination are addressed in letters. There is also an example of an actual letter used to answer a difficult wage-hour charge.

Besides giving you all these sample letters, the book also shows how to compose impressive letters of your own in the human resources area—letters that get the results you desire for your organization, not merely the attitude you should reflect or the idea you should try to convey, but the words that have proven effective in actual situations in real companies.

Often, the most difficult aspect of human resources letters is getting started. The book helps you discover how to start your own letters with these ideas.

In addition, Chapter 11 offers several special features:

- A checklist for organizing and writing business letters
- A troubleshooting guide to redundancies, intensifiers, and dead wood
- A cliché survival kit
- A communications guideline for avoiding bias in writing—a problem that personnel managers can't afford to overlook

Another special feature is the "Manager's Tips" section in each chapter, which tells the type of environment you are in when writing, for example, a letter on company benefits: you are in a marketing mode, but can't be self-serving. Your objective is to write a memorandum or letter on this subject so that the employee is aware of the good benefits you have, but is not turned off to your message.

These "Manager's Tips" ensure that you will know the key issues in each of the personnel areas and be able to incorporate the most effective ingredients so that you will send the letter that will get the results you want every time.

The *Portfolio* also does the following:

- Tells you how to gather the facts you need and establish priorities for them. It tells how to put yourself in the readers' position and how to write personnel letters simply and naturally.
- Gives you original beginnings on various subjects that capture your readers' attention immediately and keep them reading on. It tells you how to use beginnings, summary beginnings, and question beginnings to stir interest.
- Includes 15 important letter-writing tips and covers the politics of letters and how they affect your personnel and human resources relationships.
- Addresses the problems of bias in letters and shows how to avoid sex and racial bias in your writing.
- Provides, in addition to the types of letters previously cited, letters dealing with labor relations, plant closings, and layoffs.

The *Portfolio* covers nearly every personnel-related situation you will encounter and gives alternative letters on several subjects.

The letters will work equally well in organizations of various sizes—small, medium, and large. The broad scope of the book includes actual letters that have produced positive results for such organizations as Union Pacific Corporation, Gates Corporation, Manville Corporation, Baldwin United, Security Life, United Bank of Littleton, Colorado, and many other companies.

With all these models to choose from, you don't have to waste time composing letters suitable for each occasion. Simply scan the Table of Contents or the Letter Locater Index for the appropriate sample and dictate it for a quick, effective response. The *Portfolio* will save you so much time you will wonder what you ever did without it.

Mary F. Cook

Table of Contents

Review by the OFCCP Has Been Completed • To Vice-President Reviewing the Affirmative Action Progress of the Company • To U.S. Department of Labor, Office of Federal Contract Compliance Programs Regarding Minority Vendor Program • To Supervisors Regarding Sexual Harassment Policy • To Department Heads Regarding Sexual Harassment • To Managers Regarding Workshop on Awareness of Sexual Harassment • To U.S. Department of Labor, Office of Federal Contract Compliance Programs Concerning Request for Delay of Desk Audit • Informing Employees About Equal Employment Opportunity Policy (Three Samples) • To Managers Providing Affirmative Action Update • To Managers Regarding Affirmative Action Workshop

Letter Locater Index

Find It Quickly Under the Addressee-Identifier Groupings

LETTERS TO REGULATORY EXECUTIVES—EEO, CIVIL RIGHTS, OSHA, WAGE HOUR, WORKER'S COMPENSATION, UNEMPLOYMENT COMPENSATION, ETC.

LETTERS TO COMMUNITY OFFICIALS

LETTERS TO OUTSIDE ORGANIZATIONS AND UNIVERSITIES

LETTERS TO EMPLOYEES

LETTERS TO EMPLOYEES (cont'd.)

LETTERS TO EXECUTIVES, VICE-PRESIDENTS, PRESIDENTS, ETC.

LETTERS TO EXECUTIVES, VICE-PRESIDENTS, PRESIDENTS, ETC. (cont'd.)

LETTERS TO MANAGERS AND OTHER PROFESSIONALS

LETTERS TO MANAGERS AND OTHER PROFESSIONALS (cont'd.)

LETTERS TO EMPLOYEES, APPLICANTS, AND OTHERS OFFERING CONGRATULATIONS, CONDOLENCES, THANK YOUS

LETTERS TO APPLICANTS

LETTERS TO VENDORS

LETTERS FROM PERSONNEL RECRUITERS TO APPLICANTS

1

Letters That Facilitate
Recruiting and Selection

Letters that help you select and hire the most productive people in every area of your company are letters that appeal to today's workers. According to surveys done by the New York attitude research firm of Yankelovich, Skelly & White, the "new values" of workers will force major changes in personnel selection systems, compensation and benefit packages, equal employment issues, human resource development, and labor relations in the next ten years.

The hidden contract that younger workers bring to their jobs is quite different from that of over-35 workers, and it is not likely to be tempered much by poor economic conditions.

Under-35 workers, the baby-boom generation who will make up about half the work force in the 1980s, have no memory of the Depression of the 1930s and so their psychology of entitlement is different. The good life is perceived as owed, not earned, and a well-paid job is a birthright.

Women's goals, which had focused almost entirely on the family, are today quite different. More women are seeking self-fulfillment through long-term careers, and more women are reading ads looking for jobs. If your ads or letters are loaded with bias, women will spot it and avoid your jobs and your products.

For most of these people, this focus on individual needs takes the form of a search for personal growth, psychic reward, and the challenge of a stimulating career. If an organization is to attract these new workers, it must be through an awareness of the types of advertisements they will relate to. The organization's environment must be structured to attract and retain these workers; compensation, benefits, and programs such as flexible benefits, flexible hours, and child care (to name a few) will be needed. People will relate to the organizations that relate to them, and the recruiting and selection programs must reflect an up-to-date image of our times. Letters are a symbol of an organization's culture.

This chapter includes a wide variety of recruiting and selection letters written in a style that will attract or retain the productive workers you need to make your organization an economic success.

MANAGER'S TIPS FOR RECRUITING AND SELECTION LETTERS

- Tone and style should reflect an open, pro-active organizational culture where an applicant could expect to find a challenging career.

- Letters replying to applicants saying there are no jobs should be honest and considerate of the applicants. Don't use stilted or trite language.

- In all recruiting letters, use the same words you'd use if you were talking to an applicant. Avoid pompous sentences.

- Letters to outside recruiters, relocation companies, colleges, and the like, should be short and to the point. Set out details, then sum up your purpose at the end.

CONFIRMATION OF JOB OFFER

Mr. John M. Mason
793 Iris Street
Denver, Colorado 80213

Dear John:

We are pleased to confirm an offer of employment as a Mining Engineer with West Slope Energy Company, at an annual salary of $43,000, effective September 1, 19——, your first day of employment.

We feel your experience will provide needed expertise in our Engineering Department and, in turn, believe the company can provide you with opportunities for personal and professional growth.

Please come to the Personnel Department for a New Employee Orientation at 8:00 A.M., September 1. We will explain your benefits and assist you in completing your employment processing.

We are pleased that you have chosen our company and look forward to having you commence employment. Please contact me if there is anything further I can do to assist you—welcome to West Slope Energy Company.

Sincerely,

John L. Simons

APPLICANT ACCEPTANCE LETTER

Mr. Arturo M. Rodriguez
1933 McPhail Street
Memphis, Tennessee 48260

Dear Mr. Rodriguez:

The United Bank of Littleton is pleased that you have accepted our offer of the vice president position at $40,000 per year. As previously discussed, you will receive a performance review in six months and salary consideration after twelve months of employment.

In addition to this, the Bank will pay for the normal and reasonable movement of your household goods. We will also pay for you to drive your car, with your spouse, to Denver. When the time comes for you to move your household goods, we will pay for the air fare to Memphis in order for you to finalize your move, and your return trip to bring your second car to Denver. In an effort to offset additional expenses, we will reimburse up to $1,000 for various relocation-related matters. This should include additional trips for you and/or your spouse, as well as temporary lodging. We would expect these expenses to be in compliance with the normal and reasonable relocation guidelines.

You will be expected to sign a non-interest-bearing note for the total moving expenses. The note will be for twenty-four (24) months with ¼4th of this to be expensed by the Bank each month. Should you choose to leave the Bank before the completion of the 24-month period, the balance of the note would be due and payable by you.

We are very happy to have you become a member of what we consider to be the finest financial institution in the state, United Banks of Colorado, Inc. The skills and knowledge you will bring with you will be a definite asset to our organization. We look forward to seeing you on Friday, the first of July. You should report to my office at 9:00 A.M.

Please review this letter and return it with your signature by Friday, June 10.

If you should have any questions, please do not hesitate to call me at (303) 794-4291.

Sincerely yours,

Edwin J. Quinn
Assistant Vice-President
   and Personnel Manager

AGREED TO AND ACCEPTED BY:

_____

Arturo M. Rodriguez

Dated: _____

RELOCATION CONFIRMATION

CONFIDENTIAL

   TO: Arturo M. Rodriguez
FROM: Edwin Quinn
DATE: May 31, 19——
 SUBJ: NOTE FOR RELOCATION EXPENSES
_____

This memorandum is intended to confirm our agreement to have you sign a non-interest-bearing note, amortized over a twenty-four (24)-month period for a total of $5,000 for moving expenses. The total amount will be reduced by ¼4th for each month of your initial twenty-four months of employment beginning July 1, 19——. Should you voluntarily terminate employment with the United Bank of Littleton during this initial twenty-four-month period, the balance will be due and payable on demand.

_____	Date
Arturo M. Rodriguez	
_____	Date
Edwin J. Quinn	

RELOCATION SERVICE LETTER

Mr. John H. Stephens
Vice-President, Human Resources
Computer Technology Resources, Inc.
4500 Arrowhead Drive
Carson City, Nevada 89701

Dear John:

As you know we have been using Mid-America Relocation Services since 19——, to handle relocation of both newly hired and transferred employees.

In the last 18 months we have been experiencing service and billing problems and our efforts to correct the problems have failed.

We have scheduled a meeting with executives of Mid-America and with executives of our divisional headquarters here in Denver. I would appreciate it if you would attend that meeting. It will be held in our offices in Denver on October 27th. By attending you will hear about the problems firsthand and perhaps have some new ideas for an effective solution.

If we do not reach a solution in the near future, I plan to recommend we change relocation services.

I will make reservations for you at the Ramada Inn on I-70 and Kipling and will meet you the morning of the 27th for breakfast to go over our files.

If you cannot attend the meeting please let me know by October 21st.

Sincerely,

Fred M. Linquist
Personnel Manager

EXPLANATION OF MORTGAGE INTEREST DIFFERENTIAL ALLOWANCE

Mr. Ronald A. Woods
34422 N.E. 7th Avenue
North Miami, Florida 33161

Dear Ron:

You asked for an explanation of the company policy on mortgage interest differential allowance. I am sending you a complete copy of our relocation policy, which includes an explanation of the allowance but will provide a shorter version in this letter so that you will have an answer as quickly as possible.

Our mortgage interest differential allowance (MIDA) is specifically designed to offset some of the increased interest expenses incurred by transferred employees. Following is our MIDA formula:

"The annual interest rate on the new mortgage (if at least two percentage points greater than the old), less the old interest rate multiplied by the old or new mortgage balance (whichever is less), multiplied by a factor of 3."

Here's an example:

	12.5%	New interest rate
−	10.0%	Old interest rate
	2.5%	Greater than 2%, therefore qualifies for MIDA
×	$60,000	Lesser of the two balances
	$ 1,500	
	× 3	
	$ 4,500	MIDA payment

The enclosed relocation policy provides in-depth information, but if you have questions please give me a call.

Best regards,

Frank M. Ammons
Relocation Manager

NEW EMPLOYEE ORIENTATION SCHEDULE

Mr. James C. Maddox
342 Magnolia Street
Denver, Colorado 80202

Dear Jim:

I am enclosing a copy of the orientation schedule for your first week of employment at Rocky Mountain Energy Company.

The orientation program has been developed to assist you in learning about the Employee Relations Department and our current projects as quickly as possible.

We are looking forward to working with you and to making your first weeks on the job productive and enjoyable.

Welcome to the company, and to the employee relations group.

Sincerely,

Mary F. Cook
Director, Employee Relations

Enc. Orientation Schedule

ORIENTATION SCHEDULE
James C. Maddox

April 11, 19—— (Monday)

8:15–10:00		New Employee Orientation
10:00–11:00	Larry White	Review of current Organizational Development activities
11:45–	John King	Lunch
1:30–2:30	Mary Cook	Review of current Employee Relations activities
2:30–3:30	John King	Overview of Recruiting, Employment, and Affirmative Action program
3:30–5:00	Dick Brown	Overview of Compensation, Benefits, Approval Package processes, etc.

April 12, 19—— (Tuesday)

8:30–noon	(Auditorium)	Attend Managers Administrative Overview presentation
Noon	(open)	Lunch
2:00–4:30	Mary Cook	Introductions around the company

April 13, 19—— (Wednesday)

8:30–10:30	Mary Cook	Discussion of Succession Planning and Management Development
11:45–	Dan Smith	Lunch
1:30–2:30	Dan Smith	Review of Training and Management Development programs planned for 19—— to 19——
2:30–5:00	(open)	

REPLIES TO APPLICANTS: SAMPLE ONE

Ms. Sheila Connors
5362 Utica
Denver, Colorado 80017

Dear Ms. Connors:

This letter will acknowledge receipt of your inquiry regarding employment opportunities with Rocky Mountain Energy Company.

We have carefully reviewed your credentials together with those of other applicants and have selected, for further consideration, an applicant whose background is more closely related to the needs of our current job requirements.

We will have another opening in about 30 days and your experience in financial planning would make you a qualified candidate for that position. As soon as that position has been approved and we commence our recruiting activities, we will give you a call.

Your interest in Rocky Mountain Energy Company is appreciated, and we hope that you will keep in touch with us.

Sincerely,

Mary F. Cook
Director, Employee Relations

REPLIES TO APPLICANTS: SAMPLE TWO

Mr. Stephen L. Lipscomb
380 South Corona
Albuquerque, New Mexico 87108

Dear Mr. Lipscomb:
Thank you for your inquiry regarding our advertisement for a Plant Manager.

Although we are impressed with your abilities and accomplishments, we have filled the position with another candidate whose experience is better suited to our current needs. The information you submitted will be retained for one year, and you will be contacted if an appropriate position becomes available within that time.

Your interest in New Mexico Equipment Company is very much appreciated.

Sincerely,

Ruth L. Aspen
Employment Manager

REPLIES TO APPLICANTS: SAMPLE THREE

Mr. Daniel M. Norton
10840 Foothill Road
Golden, Colorado 80401

Dear Mr. Norton:
Thank you for your inquiry regarding employment opportunities with the Lawless Construction Company.

Unfortunately, we do not anticipate any openings for construction workers at the time you expect to graduate. However, the information that you submitted will be retained for one year, and you will be contacted should an appropriate position open within the next 12 months.

Your interest in our Company is appreciated, and we wish you success in your job search.

Sincerely,

James C. Wade
Personnel Manager

REPLIES TO APPLICANTS: SAMPLE FOUR

Mr. Kyle D. Morris
24 South Watson
Golden, Colorado 80401

Dear Kyle:

Thank you for sending your résumé and your letter of August 1, in which you ask us to consider you for employment.

I wish I had good news and could say that we had some openings at the present time, but two weeks ago we had a layoff that included several geologists, and at the current time we have no openings.

I would like to compliment you, however, on your cover letter. It was sincere, well written, and would earn you an interview if we had an opening. If I can be of any assistance and it would be helpful to talk to someone in the mining industry, I would be glad to take time to talk with you if you want to give me a call.

Sincerely,

Neil Thompson
Personnel Director

P.S. I am enclosing a packet that we gave to our people who were laid off, to assist them in their job search. You may find something useful in this packet.

REPLIES TO APPLICANTS: SAMPLE FIVE

Mr. R. O. Hibler
639 North Miller Drive
Salt Lake City, Utah 84120

Dear Mr. Hibler:

Your letter to Mr. James C. Wilson, president of Rocky Mountain Energy Company, regarding employment opportunities with our company has been referred to me for response.

Your skills and background are impressive; however, at this time we do not have an open position that would fit your qualifications. We will keep your résumé on file and will contact you if an applicable opening should occur.

In the meantime, another possibility might be our corporate audit staff. If you are interested, you may contact or send your résumé to Mr. Charles Billing, Assistant Controller, Union Pacific Corporation, 1416 Dodge Street, Omaha, Nebraska 68179.

Thank you for your interest in Rocky Mountain Energy Company, and please feel free to keep in touch with us.

Sincerely,

Mary F. Cook
Director, Employee Relations

cc: James C. Wilson
    President

THANK YOU FOR AN APPLICANT REFERRAL

Ms. Stacy Rundell
Administrative Assistant
SERI
10136 Nineteenth Avenue
Lakewood, Colorado 80215

Dear Stacy:

Thank you for sending the résumé on Ruth Lopez, who is currently manager of Public Affairs at ANAMEK. Ms. Lopez certainly has excellent background and experience.

Although we have no openings in either Public or Community Affairs at present, I am sending the résumé to the managers of each of those departments for their future information. Occasionally our managers know of other openings in the mining industry. If they do know of any openings in her field, we'll give her a call.

Thanks for your interest in Rocky Mountain Energy Company.

Sincerely,

Mary F. Cook
Director, Employee Relations

ASKING EMPLOYEE TO RECONSIDER RELOCATION

Mr. John C. Laman
65340 Applewood Lane
Golden, Colorado 80401

Dear John:

I would like to urge you to reconsider your decision not to accept a transfer to the San Antonio office. Because of that area's potential for low-cost coal reserves, it will be receiving a large portion of the coal department's exploration budget. As we discussed previously, your two-year involvement in our South Texas exploration program makes your experience more valuable to the company if it can be utilized in that area.

The Denver district exploration office is fully staffed to handle all current and future work assignments, and there are no openings at the present time. In light of this, and in consideration of our objectives, this transfer would be the most beneficial use of your experience.

John, I must repeat, as a senior member of the Texas exploration team, your presence in the San Antonio office is absolutely necessary.

We will do everything possible to make this transfer easy for you and your family by providing payment of all relocation costs, home purchase agreements and contracts, and in addition, we will provide a $3,000 relocation bonus. You will receive a 10 percent increase in your current salary as a cost-of-living adjustment.

Please indicate to me in writing no later than April 28 your acceptance or refusal of this transfer.

Sincerely,

Janice L. Browne
Personnel Manager

CONFIRMATION OF TRANSFER DECISION

Mr. John L. Duncan
10120 West 20th Avenue
Lakewood, Colorado 80215

Dear John:

This letter will confirm our offer to you of a transfer to our California facility at Santa Clara.

The transfer will include the following benefits:

Salary increase from $38,000 per year to $42,000 per year.

Company car—your choice of any mid-size model to be picked up on your arrival at our facility on November 28.

A relocation bonus of $3,000 to cover any out-of-pocket expenses.

Full relocation benefits, including buy-out of your current home through Trans America Relocation Services and assistance in buying a new home of similar cost. You will receive a mortgage interest rate differential payment if there is an increase in the interest rate between your old loan and the new loan.

Ralph Loomis will be your transfer and relocation contact in our personnel department. Please let him know what make of car you decide on, and give him an idea of your timing on all relocation matters. You can reach him at (303) 278-4462. You can count on him to handle all matters relative to your transfer.

I know you will enjoy your new job and the location. Santa Clara is a beautiful area. If you should have any problems at all, please give me a call; we want this transfer to be a positive experience for you and your family.

Sincerely,

Ned F. Gilbert
General Manager

CONFIRMATION OF TERMS OF RELOCATION COSTS

Mr. Jerome Little
Vice President, Mining Operations
Aspen Creek Coal Company
Post Office Box 2000
Durango, Colorado 81303

Dear Jerome:

As agreed in our discussion on April 27, any Aspen Creek hourly employee who is offered an employment transfer to the Western States Mining Company, or any of our other operations, will be reimbursed a maximum of $1,000 for all allowable relocation expenses. These expenses will be reimbursed to the employee upon presentation of valid receipts. Allowable expenses are:

1. Mileage for up to two vehicles in moving to the new location.
2. Temporary living expenses at the new location, limited to actual room costs plus taxes and meals, for up to 30 days. The maximum reimbursement for meals per day, including taxes and tips, will be:
   $20.00—employee only
   $35.00—employee with spouse
   $15.00—per child
3. Transportation of household goods.

4. Transportation of mobile home, to include those costs lised on the attached addendum.

5. Three 8-hour days with pay for relocation.

Further, relocation expenses reimbursed to those Aspen Creek employees transferred to Western States will be charged to Aspen Creek's relocation budget.

Sincerely,

Charles Ewing
Personnel Manager

CONGRATULATIONS ON REASSIGNMENT

Mr. Frank Uzelli
6400 West 20th Avenue
Minneapolis, Minnesota 55426

Dear Mr. Uzelli:

Congratulations on your recent reassignment. I'm sure your new job will give you added opportunities for career development and growth, and at the same time allow you to utilize fully your current expertise.

I am attaching a summary of our relocation policy which will be of assistance to you in your move to Spokane. The details are easily understood, but I know you will have specific questions. Please give me a call after you've had a chance to read the policy.

An Approval Form for Estimated Expenses and Allowances is enclosed for your completion. Estimates called for on the form should reflect your best guess as to expenses you expect to incur. Please complete this form, have your supervisor sign it, and return it to me as quickly as possible.

At your earliest opportunity, please contact Jan Browne in our Purchasing Department to discuss the movement of your household belongings, and to gain her assistance in obtaining an estimated cost for the shipment of your household goods.

Also attached is a Request for Reimbursement of Moving Expenses form for itemizing your relocation expenses. Receipts are required for air travel, lodging, car rental, and any other out-of-pocket expenses exceeding $25. Please use a separate form for each type of expense.

Please call if you have a question or if I may be of further assistance with your relocation. My office extension is 415.

Sincerely,

Charles Ewing
Personnel Manager

JOB-SHARING PROPOSAL: SAMPLE ONE

Mr. Franklin T. Thompson
General Manger
Micro Computer Corporation
6365 Mariposa Street
San Francisco, California 94101

Dear Frank:

We've discussed the pros and cons of instituting a job-sharing program on several occasions. Because of a shortage of computer programmers I would like to try a job-sharing program on a trial basis.

Four women have contacted us about job sharing. They live in the general area of our new facility and had heard that we needed programmers. We have checked their references and find they have good recommendations from their former employers. None of the four wants to work full time because each has small children.

We would like to try the job-sharing arrangement with these four women. They have worked out their work and babysitting schedules and the schedules fit our needs. I recommend a six-month trial period.

I realize there will be increased benefit costs in some areas because we will have four people on the payroll instead of two, but we are experiencing such a shortage of programmers that I feel the increase in benefit costs is acceptable.

Please let me know what you think. I'd like to start the program on June 13, 19——

Best regards,

Dianne K. Miller
Personnel Manager

JOB-SHARING PROPOSAL: SAMPLE TWO

Mr. L. M. Yates
Vice-President
Harding-Snelling, Inc.
3042 Simms Street
Lakewood, Colorado 80215

Dear Larry:

Some companies have started using a concept of job design that takes advantage of complementary skills of more than one employee to carry out a specific job function. We have initiated the job-sharing concept for various reasons. One is to accommodate the needs of a valued employee or employees, as well as provide added know-how for selected high-demand jobs as in the data processing field.

It is recommended that two candidates fill the position of Data Technician in the Coal Evaluation Department. These two candidates are Debra Johnson and Gloria Mooton. They have expressed their desire to move from the full-time status to permanent part-time. Both women have the technical expertise the company needs.

Should the position of Data Technician be shared by these two individuals on a part-time basis, each would work 24 hours per week. It is expected that both the quality and quantity of work output will be met, if not improved.

The position involves the collation of large amounts of data into a sensible, workable system. It is, at times, a tedious function that calls for the transferring of data collected in the field onto the computer, and then updating and correcting the computer files on a continuous basis. Over the past two years, the tasks of the technician have grown tremendously. The additional eight hours of work per week, along with the reduced hours per day per individual (six) should increase productivity and improve work flow efficiency.

The scheduling of overlapping hours and the fact that Gloria and Debbie both have good communication skills will assist them in attaining the needed additional coordination that will be required to effectively do the job. There is an anticipated increase in employee benefit costs, because the company will have to furnish benefits for two people instead of one person, but I feel the benefits outweigh the added costs.

We will monitor the effectiveness of this new job-sharing arrangement and keep you apprised.

Sincerely,

Linda M. Lancer
Personnel Manager

VERIFICATION OF ACADEMIC DEGREE

Mr. Fred J. Speer
Vice-President, Employee Relations
Hamilton Technology Corporation
Ten Energy Place
Denver, Colorado 80202

Dear Fred:

In an effort to avoid a recurrence of the recent problems associated with the lack of verification of the academic degree of an applicant, the following practices are being instituted.

Recruiting sources, such as employment agencies and executive search firms, will be required to verify degrees listed by applicants by providing Hamilton Technology Corporation a verified copy of the college transcript.

Applicants resulting from our direct recruiting and advertising activities who are among the final candidates for a position will sign a release form enabling us to request college transcripts. A telephone verification of degrees earned will be made on final candidates for whom we have not yet received written documentation at the time an employment offer is to be made.

Additionally, our Application for Employment form, which is being revised, will carry a statement in the Education section stating, "This information requires documented verification."

In summary, prior to extending an offer of employment to any candidate, we will ensure that we have verified all degree-related information in addition to the normal prior-employment reference checks.

Sincerely,

Jan C. Blake
Personnel Manager

SUMMER EMPLOYMENT: SAMPLE ONE

Mr. James C. Stilwell
President
Stilwell Manufacturing Company
Post Office Box 3000
Arvada, Colorado 80004

Dear Mr. Stilwell:

A total of 55 temporary summer employees were hired during 19———. This included 15 females and one minority. The average age of summer employees was 21, and the average amount of education was 14.5 years.

Thirty-six of the students attend colleges in Colorado and Wyoming; 19 are residents of other states. The program lasted a total of 22 weeks.

The average salary was $833.70 per month. Nine part-time summer employees were paid $3.00 per hour. Our total salary expense for summer employees was $105,423.69. Add to that overtime pay of $18,742.95 and business expenses and cash advances of $77,389.40, for a total expenditure of $201,556.04, or an average of $3,664.65 per student.

One employee, who will complete his undergraduate degree in December, has been extended an offer as an Entry Level Mine Engineer. One Entry Level Land Representative was hired through the program, as well as two Reclamation Technicians and five Field Geologists who were retained at the end of the summer in temporary positions.

Sincerely,

Edith L. Decker
Director of Employment

SUMMER EMPLOYMENT: SAMPLE TWO

Summer Placement Program
Placement Office
Utah University
Salt Lake City, Utah 84112

Attention: Placement Officer

The Utah Construction Company plans to have approximately 37 summer jobs on the new state highway project. The work begins June 4th and will be regularly scheduled through September 10th, when the project will be winding down.

Please advise students who are interested in heavy construction work for the summer that the hourly rate will be $12.00 per hour and there will be some overtime, which will be paid at time-and-a-half.

Interested students should write to:

Lane Wilkerson
P.O. Box 548
Salt Lake City, Utah 84112

Sincerely,

Scott T. White
Personnel Manager

SUMMER EMPLOYMENT: SAMPLE THREE

Mr. Larry J. Blankenship
P.O. Box 732
Golden, Colorado 80401

Dear Mr. Blankenship:

Thank you for your inquiry regarding summer employment opportunities at the Computer Technology Corporation.

Your qualifications have been carefully evaluated with regard to our summer employment needs; unfortunately, a position commensurate with your background and interests is not available. We may have an opening approximately July 1st, and you would be eligible to apply if you are available at that time.

We will retain your résumé. Please call us sometime around the end of June if you are still interested in a position.

Your interest in our company is appreciated and we wish you success in finding a summer job.

Sincerely,

Richard L. Williams
Employment Manager

COURTESY LETTER REGARDING
A SUMMER EMPLOYEE

Mr. James L. Bowen
President
Hamilton, Bowen & Associates
345 Park Avenue
New York, New York 10022

Dear Jim:

I thought you might like to know how Kris Minton, the young man you referred to us for a summer job, has done in our summer student program.

Kris worked in our marketing department performing various duties, but primarily in the area of market research, working with Steve Meyers. Kris contributed significantly to the Foothills project and did a fine job. We are impressed with his abilities and enthusiasm and will retain him on a part-time basis during the school year.

We appreciate your referring Kris to us.

Best regards,

David J. Gilbert
Director Human Resources

CAMPUS RECRUITING LETTER

Mr. James C. Pleninger
Recruiting Advisor
University of Denver
Denver, Colorado 80207

Dear Mr. Pleninger:

I will be coming to your campus for the purpose of recruiting business, accounting, and finance students on May 5, 19——.

I would like to meet with you that morning, if possible, and will call you on Monday, May 2nd, for an appointment.

We are always favorably impressed with the students we interview at Denver University, and I look forward to another recruiting effort and working with you and your staff.

Best regards,

Lincoln M. Barton
Manager,
Recruiting and Selection

"THANK YOU" FOR INTERVIEW OF A FRIEND

Mrs. Laura Johnson
Personnel Manager
Harding-Smelling, Inc.
3042 Simms Street
Lakewood, Colorado 80215

Dear Laura:

Thank you for taking the time to do an informational interview for Carl Higginson. Carl is looking for a position as an operations manager and although you had no openings at the time, I know he was grateful for your time and the referral you provided.

I read in the <u>Denver Post</u> last Sunday that your company has had a nice increase in earnings. Congratulations! I know that your good efforts in the personnel area contributed to that increase.

I'd like to buy you lunch and will call you next week to check your schedule.

Sincerely,

Jean Hunt

PERSONNEL RECRUITER LETTER
TO APPLICANT: SAMPLE ONE

Mr. Henry P. Gordon
945 Mombo Drive
St. Louis, Missouri 63129

Dear Mr. Gordon:

I enjoyed very much the chance to meet and become acquainted with you. Your background is impressive, and you can certainly be proud of your many accomplishments.

I have reviewed your background and experience with my client. Although your qualifications are excellent, they have made the difficult decision to pursue another candidate whose particular combination of skills and experience more closely fits their position.

They did, however, want me to convey their appreciation for your interest.

Let's keep in touch.

Sincerely,

STM ASSOCIATES

Donald R. Simon
Partner

**PERSONNEL RECRUITER LETTER
TO APPLICANT: SAMPLE TWO**

Mr. Pierce M. Gordon
8534 Montgomery Avenue
New York, New York 10012

Dear Mr. Gordon:

We received your résumé, and find your experience and accomplishments interesting.

In order that we might have a more complete assessment of your background, I would appreciate receiving some additional information. Please feel free to respond on this correspondence and return it in the enclosed prepaid envelope.

- What are your salary objectives and history?
- What type of position are you seeking?
- What are your location preferences?
- Why are you considering a change?
- How did you hear of STM?

When we receive a position paralleling your background and interests, we will contact you. I look forward to receiving this information.

Thank you for your interest in STM.

Sincerely,

STM ASSOCIATES

Donald R. Simon
Partner

**PERSONNEL RECRUITER LETTER
TO APPLICANT: SAMPLE THREE**

Ms. Julie F. McCauley
475 Lincoln Lane
Denver, Colorado 80211

Dear Julie:

Acme Minerals Company has made a final selection for the mining engineer position. The individual has not yet given notice, so I cannot mention a name at this time.

The choice was difficult, since all the candidates were well qualified. The selection resulted in a close match between the position specifications and the individual's background.

I have enjoyed working with you on this assignment, and will certainly keep you apprised of future positions. Also, please let me know of new developments with your career so I may better evaluate opportunities as they arise.

Sincerely,

STM ASSOCIATES

Donald R. Simon
Partner

INFORMATION ON RECRUITING BROCHURE

Mr. J. F. Allen
J. F. Allen Associates
13601 Colorado Boulevard
Denver, Colorado 80223

Dear John:

Attached is a rough draft of the recruiting brochure I mentioned on the phone. We'd like to have the same type of pamphlet we've had before (sample attached), but jazz it up a bit—maybe use an employee picture collage to put our employees in the spotlight.

The recruiting pamphlet is used inside a folder, so the size of the old pamphlet is fine. It would be better to have the printing at the top so that it stands out from the short flap on the folder. Perhaps the picture collage could appear on the bottom. We would like to use new colors and would appreciate your suggestions.

After you have had a chance to review the old brochure, please give me a call so we can get together to finalize the details.

Please say hello to Ellen. Joan and I enjoyed having dinner with the two of you at the United Way banquet last Saturday evening.

Best wishes,

Lawrence T. Wexler
Personnel Manager

RECRUITING AND RELOCATION BUDGET

Mr. David E. Hicks
Manager, Strategic Planning
Rocky Mountain Energy
P.O. Box 2000
Broomfield, Colorado 80020

Dear Mr. Hicks:

In response to your request for recruiting and relocation information to be used in preparing the 19—— budget, the following data is provided:

<u>Recruiting Costs</u> (all of 19—— and 19——)
- Average recruiting cost per exempt position filled $ 4,106.26
- Average recruiting cost per nonexempt position filled   400.90
- Average recruiting cost per hourly position filled   224.00

<u>Relocation Costs</u> (all of 19—— and 19——)
- Average cost per exempt relocation $18,172.95
- Average cost per nonexempt relocation   5,744.50
- Average cost per relocation—homeowner   20,531.71

If you have any questions or require any further information or assistance, please call me.

Sincerely,

Mel Dunham
Employment Manager

NEW EMPLOYEE WELCOME

Ms. Joan Purcell
17054 32nd Avenue
Golden, Colorado 80401

Dear Joan:

Welcome to Front Range Energy Corporation. We are looking forward to working with you and hope you will enjoy your part-time position with our company. You'll want to review our <u>Things to Know</u> guidelines covered in the enclosure.

FREC is the mineral resources exploration and development subsidiary of the National Energy Corporation. Other subsidiaries of National are Overland Industries and Front Range Technology Corporation.

Our organization is highly integrated and comprised of many departments, such as: Exploration, Engineering, Land Acquisition, Human Resources, Accounting, Data Processing, Drafting, Marketing, Law, Mineral Economics, and so forth. As a result, a variety of challenging opportunities are offered to those who have the skills and desire to fill our positions.

We try to provide challenging opportunities for growth for our full-time employees and as these full-time positions become available, we welcome your application for employment. Should you decide to seek permanent employment at Front Range Energy Corporation, you may contact our human resources department and a staff member will be pleased to discuss career opportunities with you.

Sincerely,

Fred M. Pruett
Director of Human Resources
Enc. <u>Things to Know</u>

Things to Know

- You were called in for an important job—one that no one else can do at this time. We are counting on you to get the job done. If you perform your job well, you will be contributing significantly to the accomplishment of our goals.

  If you have any questions about the work you are doing, please do not hesitate to ask your supervisor. If you have questions your supervisor cannot answer, contact the Employee Relations Department.

- Employees are expected to dress in suitable office attire. Our image is reflected by the people who work here, and our work, actions, and appearance are important.

- Parking. Please use the employees' parking lot on the north side of the building. Do not use spaces marked "Van Pool Parking."

- Our work hours are 8:00 A.M. to 5:00 P.M.

- Lunch is normally from 12:00 noon to 1:00 P.M. A cafeteria is located on the second level on the west side of the building.

- We do not have set break periods. We know that you need a "breather" now and then and hope you will take one when needed.

  There is free coffee, hot chocolate, and tea in the galley. Ask your supervisor or co-workers where the nearest galley is located. Vending machines are located on the west end of the first level.

- We realize that there are times when personal calls are necessary. However, we would appreciate it if you would keep them to a minimum. Dial 9 to get an outside line.

- Make sure you complete the time slip provided by your agency at the end of your assignment, or at the end of each week, and have your supervisor sign it. Then, send a copy of the signed time slip to Employee Relations.

About Typing

- Attached is a sample letter and a memo that show the format that is used company-wide. Ask about special formats used within the departments.

- Proofread all typing that you do. Errors must be corrected. If your errors are obvious, please do the letter or memo over again. Clean and neat typing is important!

- Make sure all spelling and grammar are accurate. If you are not sure, ask your supervisor.

- The following copies are needed for every letter and memo:
  a. original
  b. department file copy
  c. originator's personal copy (optional)

- Be aware of what you are typing. If the material is confidential, please treat it that way.

- Copying machines are located throughout the building. Ask your supervisor where the nearest one is located.

Answering the Telephone

- Ask your supervisor about special procedures within the department.
- When taking messages, record the caller's full name, company, telephone number, and message. On the message slip, write your name, the date, and the time the person called.
- Most departments have designated message centers. If not, leave the message in an obvious place so the employee can return the call.
- If you receive an urgent call for an employee who is in a meeting, take the message and place the caller on hold. Then take the message to the employee at the meeting.
- If your job does not entail answering the telephone, please do so if no one else is available and follow the steps outlined above.
- In all cases, please be courteous to those who call.

If any other questions arise that these instructions do not answer, please ask your supervisor or someone in the Employee Relations Department. We want to help you do your job well so that you may enjoy your time with us.

2

Letters on Compensation Programs, Salary Surveys, and Merit Budgets

Compensation is a responsibility that so directly affects the economic results of the organization that all letters on the subject need to be crisp, clear, businesslike, and to the point. Top executives who read your letters on the subject of compensation should get a feeling that you are on top of the problems. Your letters in this area go a long way toward establishing your credibility in a key function that impacts "the bottom line."

If your letters on this subject do not give the reader a feeling of solid credibility, the entire personnel function will be questioned.

MANAGER'S TIPS ON COMPENSATION LETTERS

- It is important to build your vocabulary in the compensation area. If you do not use and understand the precise terminology, your letters will suffer.

- Executives expect you to be like their attorneys in the compensation area. Here you can be more expansive, not so laid back in style, because in this area you are talking "Big Dollars," and people want to feel your knowledge and ability.

- Letters to employees, however, should take on the tone of advisor. You need the skill of explaining compensation in such a way that you gain employees' confidence. They need to understand what you say, and feel you are leveling with them.

- Letters to field locations should not "talk down" to employees or management. Just because people are in outlying locations doesn't mean they are country bumpkins! You have to build your credibility with field personnel also.

- Letters to joint venture partners must take on a conciliatory tone. You do not have the authority to order, only to offer advice and share information.

- Letters to corporate headquarters regarding compensation or approvals of merit budgets should include *valid data* on what other similar organizations are doing, and use of a factual, logical style works best.

APPROVAL OF SALARY INCREASE BUDGETS

Ralph F. Stevens
President
Monford Energy Company
127 South Main
Casper, Wyoming 82604

Dear Ralph:

This year we are planning to accelerate the Executive Compensation Committee approval of the 19—— salary increase budgets and policy lines to September or October, at the latest. In prior years, salary budgets and policy lines were approved at the November Committee meeting. The acceleration will provide additional time for development of the 19—— salary increase program and the incorporation of such programs into our 19—— Operating Budget.

Hay Associates has assured us that their compensation survey data will be available in the first week of August. You should plan on presenting your 19—— budget and policy line recommendations to Corporate Employee Relations in August.

Upon reaching agreement with the Operating companies, we will present budget and policy line recommendations to the Office of the Chairman in September and to the Executive Compensation Committee no later than October.

A copy of your 19—— salary increase program should be submitted to me in December in order that I may review your program to assure that the Corporate objectives will be met.

This is an ambitious schedule, but we believe every effort should be made to improve the budgeting and compensation process, and with your assistance, we are confident it can be achieved. My staff will be available to work directly with your compensation group to insure a continuing and close working relationship on all of these matters.

Sincerely,

Global Energy Company, Inc.

Kurt M. Yates
President

TO MANAGERS REGARDING SALARY RECOMMENDATIONS

> TO: All Managers
> FROM: T. M. Norgren
> SUBJ: 19—— SALARY APPROVALS

The attached salary recommendations have been approved for implementation. Copies have been forwarded to the responsible vice presidents and to the appropriate manager. Additional copies of the approved salary recommendations are available to managers desiring a complete set for their areas of responsibility.

To effect January and February salary actions, it is important to submit individual performance appraisals and computer profiles to me by December 20. January 1 increases will appear in the January 20 paycheck. Reminders will also be given for increases occurring through the rest of the year.

Supervisors and managers are authorized to approve the computer profiles if the increase is the same as approved on the attached sheets. One-up approval is required if the original recommendation is modified but is still within policy. All other changes should be reviewed with me to ensure that proper approval procedures are followed.

Please call if you have any questions.

REQUEST FOR APPROVAL OF SALARY ACTIONS

Mr. James L. Gates
President
Gates Oil & Gas Corporation
372 Madison Avenue
New York, New York 10022

Dear Jim:

Your assent is requested to the following salary actions:

The transfer of Leonard Cavanagh from the position of strategic planner to director of acquisitions. In this capacity, he will head our acquisition efforts, including determining which companies qualify for consideration, developing recommendations for acquisition and financial terms, coordinating the initial transactions, and ensuring a smooth transition once an acquisition is consummated.

This position is of critical importance to the success of our strategic objectives, and I feel it qualifies for executive-level status. Mr. Cavanagh's former position in strategic planning was assigned 1500 points. I recommend that a 1700-point evaluation be approved for Mr. Cavanagh as director of acquisitions.

I also recommend that on February 1, 19——, the effective date of the transfer, his salary be increased from $70,000 to $79,000.

The promotion of Robert Maes from manager to director of operations will be effective March 1st. This opportunity results from the resignation of Van Aubaer to pursue his own consulting business. Mr. Maes has 15 years of operations experience, including three years with our organization. A 15 percent increase is recommended, which will result in a new salary of $67,000 effective February 16, 19——.

Supporting documentation for these promotions is attached.

Sincerely,

Bradley Dexter
Salary Administrator

SALARY INCREASE RECOMMENDATION

Mr. Jay M. Lehrer
General Manager
AeroJet Industries
110 Airport Road
Chicago, Illinois 61821

Dear Jay:

Based on our preliminary projections for the 19—— Salary Program recommendations, we would advise the use of a 10.2 percent increase factor in 19——. This figure is a weighted average that includes both merit and promotional increases. It was also computed as a time-weighted, population-weighted average that takes into account the variability of scheduled increases through the course of the year.

Please advise managers that the 10.2 percent increase should be applied equally to all January 10, 19—— effective base salaries in their departments.

Best regards,

Lane T. Voge
Compensation Manager

STATUS OF EXEMPT AND
NON-EXEMPT SALARY BUDGETS

Mr. John L. Long
Vice-President, Personnel
Louisville Manufacturing Company
Louisville, Kentucky 40218

Dear John:

The status of the exempt and non-exempt salary budgets for all actions processed through October 1, 19—— for our Collingwood Plant are as follows:

Exempt	
Allowed for year	$1,480,553
Reported as of 9/30/——	1,347,660
Remaining budgeted increases	54,300
Recommendation	64,000
Unbudgeted promotions	11,800
Non-Exempt	
Allowed for year	370,030
Reported as of 9/30/——	308,710
Remaining budgeted increases	37,080
Recommendation	21,880
Unscheduled promotions	5,560

All of our merit increases and promotions have been given, and we currently have no open positions, so there should be very limited personnel actions between now and the end of the year.

Sincerely,

Robert A. Rippey
Compensation Manager

REQUEST FOR ADDITIONAL SALARY BUDGET

Mr. William M. Haland
Vice-President, Employee Relations
Wymore Corporation
345 Park Avenue
New York, New York 10022

Dear Bill:

As we discussed on the phone, following is an update of our request for funds to supplement our 19—— salary program in order to curtail turnover in our upper- and middle-level management staff.

Since our initial proposal on June 30, our turnover situation has continued to deteriorate. Four more managers have terminated this month, bringing the total to 15 managers so far this year. The lack of any current major projects and the general slowdown of our business is most frequently given as a major consideration of those leaving. Of course, in almost every case the managers leaving have accepted more responsible positions at higher salaries. Our turnover continues at one of the highest levels in our history.

To date, with few exceptions we have been able to fill the manager vacancies internally. Our concern is that we will start losing professionals in the middle management ranks. We know that this group is also in the job market. They are also frustrated by the slowdown of activities and have been encouraged by the apparent success of the key executives who have terminated. As we noted in our initial request for supplemental funds, the actual salaries for this group have fallen behind the industry, and we do expect that we'll need a substantially larger salary budget in 19——.

Attached is an updated list of terminations. The annualized turnover is now 18.75 percent compared to 12.5 percent for 19——.

Thank you for your consideration. Please call if you need additional information.

Sincerely,

Dale L. Myers
Director, Employee Relations
Denver Division

**SPECIAL REPORT ON
SELECTED SALARY CLASSIFICATIONS**

Mr. Franklin M. Burns
Western States Land Company
One Energy Center
Denver, Colorado 80202

Dear Frank:

The Land Department Special Research Report is a study conducted by our Research Department. It has been designed to provide management with current data on salaries for selected land department classifications.

Mailed questionnaires were used in collecting the compensation data. To facilitate accurate matching of jobs by participants, job classifications were accompanied by job descriptions that appear at the end of this report. Twelve classifications were surveyed.

The data in this report was obtained from 23 companies representing the following areas: California, Colorado, Oklahoma, and Texas.

DEFINITIONS

FORMAL RATE RANGE—A formally established minimum and maximum that a company has committed, in writing, to pay for a surveyed job. Minimum and maximum of the rate range are defined as follows:

> Minimum—The lowest rate paid to an entry-level employee who is qualified to perform the minimum requirements of the job.

> Maximum—The highest rate an employee can ultimately obtain in the job under the current salary plan.

AVERAGE MINIMUM/MAXIMUM RATES—Determined by finding the sum of the minimum or maximum rates reported and dividing the sum by the number of companies reporting rate ranges. This measurement pertains only to formal rate ranges and does not necessarily indicate any actual rates presently being paid.

WEIGHTED AVERAGE—An average weighted by the number of employees reported at each rate. It is determined by multiplying each reported rate by the number of employees receiving that rate, adding the resulting products, and dividing the sum by the total number of employees for that job classification.

MIDDLE 50 PERCENT RANGE—The middle 50 percent of the rates reported when arranged in ascending order. This calculation excludes the lowest 25 percent and the highest 25 percent of the rates, therefore making it possible to compare data without regard to the influence of the extreme limits.

> 1st Quartile—The rate that occurs at the 25th percentile.

> Median—The rate that occurs in the exact middle of the distribution of rates (50th percentile).

> 3rd Quartile—The rate that occurs at the 75th percentile.

USING THE SURVEY

Survey users should not attempt to use the reported measures of central tendency as absolute compensation standards. In making the most effective use of this survey, the following comments should be carefully considered:

1. If fewer than three companies reported information for any one data line, that information was not printed in the survey. The data line will read, "Insufficient Data."

2. Many factors, such as the sample size and mix, affect the data obtained for individual job classifications. Care should be exercised in utilizing survey data, and specific results should be examined in the context of overall survey findings, sample constitution, and so on.

3. Incumbents were reported only where they spent at least 50 percent of their time in the described function. No incumbent was reported in more than one of the survey classifications.

4. All of the survey data are based on basic straight-time rates being paid to full-time employees as of the last payroll period closest to November 25, 19——. Incumbents working fewer than 35 hours per week were not included in the survey. Additional compensation, such as overtime payments, was excluded from the survey data.

5. To ensure that the confidentiality of this survey is maintained, these data are supplied with the strict understanding that all or any portion of the information will _not_ be used in any collective bargaining session or grievance proceeding.

If you have any questions about this survey, please give me a call.

Sincerely,

Karen C. Westgard
Compensation Manager

RECOMMENDED SALARY SCHEDULE
FOR SUMMER STUDENTS

Ms. Mary C. Lewis
Manager, Personnel
Waltham Manufacturing Company
Denver, Colorado 80202

Dear Mary:

The recommended schedule of summer student rates for 19—— is attached. The rates represent a 10 percent increase over 19——.

We reviewed local survey data and last year's student program, and find that our proposed 19—— salary schedule is competitive. The comments regarding salary from the 19—— students were favorable.

We are expecting the local energy industry salary structure to increase at least 10 percent; consequently, a 10 percent increase in the summer rates should keep us competitive in 19——. We will review these rates against survey data as it becomes available. Should this information appear inconsistent with our assumptions, we will adjust the rates accordingly.

Sincerely,

Linda L. Mason
Compensation and Benefits Supervisor

OUTLINE OF PROCEDURES FOR ADMITTANCE TO SPECIAL SALARY SURVEY

Mr. Robert L. Lang
Compensation Manager
Southwest Mining Company
2727 North Central Avenue
Phoenix, Arizona 85004

Dear Bob:

Following is an outline of the procedures for admission to the Salary Survey that Hay Associates, Inc., independent consultants, conduct and manage for our industry.

Admission to the Survey Group

Companies seeking admission to the survey are required to send a participant profile form to Hay Associates' Philadelphia office. These materials are duplicated and then mailed to each company that currently participates in the survey. If all companies approve the application (based on such things as product, locations, number of job matches, etc.), the company is accepted for participation. If any questions require airing before the full membership, a final decision is deferred until the annual meeting in October.

Enrollment—Job Content Data

A visit from Hay Associates is scheduled with the newly approved participant company, and usually requires one or two full days to discuss in detail the jobs to be included in the survey. The survey encompasses primarily headquarter positions from entry-level professional to the upper levels of middle management.

Job Description Preparation

A job description is prepared by the new participant company for each survey job.

Job Evaluation

Following review of the job descriptions, the positions will be evaluated by Hay Associates utilizing the Guide Chart-Profile Method of Job Evaluation.

Survey Schedule

Salary information is collected in July, and publication of the survey is scheduled for September.

Annual Meeting

The annual meeting of the survey members normally is in October. Attendance is expected because the survey will be discussed in detail. Changes for the following year will be entertained, and general business will be conducted. Members take turns hosting the meeting.

Steering Committee

A committee exists to represent the survey members throughout the year. One of its major functions is to interface with prospective participants, and members are available to discuss the survey.

If you have any questions, give me a call. A packet of information is enclosed.

Sincerely,

Wyoming Mining Corporation

Roy P. Elliston
Compensation Manager

LETTER TO VICE-PRESIDENT REGARDING PARTICIPATION IN SPECIAL SALARY SURVEY

Mr. William S. Little
Vice-President
Medical Technologies, Inc.
545 Park Avenue
New York, New York 10022

Dear Mr. Little:

Recently, we were requested to participate in a Medical Personnel Jobs Salary Survey conducted by Mountain States Employers Council. We have just obtained the results of the survey and have annotated the Survey Summary Sheets with our comparative salary ranges and actual salary data.

The minimums, midpoints, and maximums indicated on the Survey Summary Sheets are the simple averages of all the salary range structures submitted. The "Actual" represents the weighted average of all current actual salaries for each job match. The companies that participated in the survey are listed on the sheet.

This survey group is one of the most cooperative we've worked with, and we hope to participate in the same survey again next year.

Sincerely,

Wilson Browne
Compensation Manager
Denver Division

**ANSWER TO REQUEST TO JOIN
SPECIAL SALARY SURVEY**

Ms. Joan Trotta
Northern Minerals Corporation
10 South Yosemite
Englewood, Colorado 80155

Dear Joan:

Enclosed is the packet of information you requested concerning the Hay Energy
Survey. Northern Minerals would be a valuable member of the group, and I am
certain that the data members receive would be beneficial to you. In addition, the
establishment of new industry contacts is always useful.

Participation in the survey requires considerable time and effort, especially the first
year. Position descriptions will be needed for each of the positions for which you
have a comparable job. A consultant from Hay Associates will then visit you to
correlate the positions. Survey input takes place in July, with the final product in
your hands by early October. The annual follow-up meeting is scheduled for
October.

The cost of the survey last year was $2,500 per member. Like everything else, it will
probably be slightly higher in future years. The first-year charge is approximately
$4,500 more, due to the expense of the job correlation and data input.

Please call me if I can provide any additional information.

Sincerely,

Julia S. Earnest
Manager
Compensation & Benefits

**REGARDING COMPENSATION FOR LEAD WORKERS
AND RELIEF SUPERVISORS**

Mr. V. F. Robbins
General Manager
Northrup Mining Company
One Energy Plaza
Denver, Colorado 80202

>   Subject: Compensation for Lead Workers
>   and Relief Supervisors

Dear Mr. Robbins:

The following information is provided in response to your request for us to
consider alternative premium compensation methods for hourly personnel taking
on "relief supervisor" responsibilities at construction materials sites. Without

exception, all companies in the area provide an hourly premium rate of 25 cents to 50 cents per hour for all hours worked in that capacity. These companies do not differentiate between on-site and off-site projects, but pay the same premium for both situations.

I also found that there is a common practice in the sand and gravel industry to provide an extra hour of pay above and beyond the lead worker premium to hourly employees taking on relief supervisor responsibilities for extended periods of time (e.g., more than three days in succession). This extra hour of pay would be paid at the straight-time rate, rather than the overtime rate, and would recognize the probable need for a relief supervisor to arrive early and stay later than the hourly crew.

Based on this research, I would recommend that we retain the lead worker premium of 50 cents per hour at our construction materials sites. This rate appears competitive and is in line with industry practice.

Sincerely,

John W. Lipscomb
Compensation Manager

WAGE AND SALARY RECOMMENDATIONS FOR NEW OPERATION

Mr. William S. Koch
President
Amerox Corporation
700 Park Avenue
New York, New York 10022

Dear Bill:

We have completed our studies of the labor market in the Evanston, Wyoming area and have developed wage and benefits recommendations for our new sand and gravel operation.

As you know, Evanston is located in the Overthrust Belt in the southwest corner of the state. The area has been impacted significantly by oil and gas exploration, production, and construction. With the exception of skilled mechanics and electricians, there are large numbers of transient people in the area looking for work. The wages paid by the construction companies are considerably higher than those of other businesses, but we are proposing to key our wages and benefits to the two existing sand and gravel operations.

Our proposal also takes into account the fact that most employers in the Evanston area work more than a normal 40-hour week. The schedules range from 48 to 60 hours, and in some instances are guaranteed. The following structure takes into consideration both the hourly rates and overtime schedules:

Mechanic	$11.50
Crusher Operator	10.85
Heavy Equipment Operator	"
Truck Driver	9.10
Operator Trainee	"
Laborer	8.00

We do not anticipate the large amount of overtime currently being worked at other companies; therefore, our people will not earn as much on an annual basis as employees of our competitors. (This is highlighted by our bar graphs.) If this becomes a problem, we may need to review the wage structure quarterly, at least for the first year.

Please advise if you need additional information.

Sincerely,

James L. Hanson
Manager, Employee Relations

REVIEW OF WAGES AND LABOR MARKET ASSESSMENT OF NEW OPERATION

Mr. John L. Meyers
Manager, Industrial Relations
Rankin Corporation
One City Plaza
Pittsburgh, Pennsylvania 15222

Dear John:

I appreciated the opportunity to meet with you last week to review the drafts of the proposed wages and benefits to be provided at Rankin.

I have recapped the discussions and would appreciate your input if you believe my notes should be expanded upon, changed, or deleted.

Wages

- It was agreed that the next step in the development of the wage program should be a study of various labor markets to determine logical sources for employees. This should include an assessment of who is apt to be the primary competition for qualified people. For example, it was mentioned that Langston will be significantly increasing its work force at about the same time we will be hiring.
- The effective dates of the reported survey wages will be determined, and we will report what other local companies are doing in compensation and benefits.
- The bonuses paid at neighboring plants will be reviewed.

- The wages reported as negotiated under local labor agreements will be verified.
- A strategy will be developed regarding the relative competitiveness of our wage structure, and the wage structure will be reviewed and modified if necessary.

Benefits

- Medical Insurance will be the same program as at all other Rankin locations.
- The Dental Insurance eligibility period will be changed to six months.
- Short-Term Disability—the waiting period will be reduced from seven to three days.
- Long-Term Disability—the plan will continue for a maximum of five years.
- Life Insurance—it was recommended that the amount be changed from $15,000 per employee to one times annual base salary. A flat amount of insurance for everyone would cause inequity problems with management employees.

Pension

Pension formulas will be investigated and a program designed that matches the program at our other locations.

Vacations

Two weeks vacation up to five years; three weeks thereafter.

Holidays

Eleven paid holidays.

We will require a pre-employment physical examination, and will develop a policy regarding the relocation of hourly employees should the need arise.

I have attached a checklist that we found helpful when starting a new operation. Perhaps this, or a variation of it, might be useful to you. We would also be interested in reviewing the Employee Handbook at such time as a draft is available.

Again, we enjoyed having the opportunity to discuss the recommendations with you and are available if we can assist you in any way.

Sincerely,

Ruth L. Gorden
Personnel Manager

PROPOSED HOURLY WAGE INCREASE ANNOUNCEMENT

TO: William L. Bowman

FROM: Eugene Reid

SUBJ: HOURLY WAGE RATES—LANCASTER PROJECT

Our proposed hourly wage rate increase of 5.4 percent for all hourly classifications at Lancaster has been reviewed and approved.

You are hereby authorized to announce and implement the attached wage structure effective July 1, 19——.

The recommended increase of 3.5 percent, effective January 1, 19——, was also approved subject to survey and review of the local wage situation again in the fall to assure our competitive position.

In light of our profit improvement program, it will be expected that efforts will continue to be made in increasing productivity to help offset the cost of these competitive wage increases.

AUTHORIZATION FOR HOURLY WAGE ADJUSTMENT

Mr. James L. Gates
General Manager
Conway Mining Company
4704 Harlan Street
Denver, Colorado 80212

Dear Jim:

I have received your proposed rate increases at Lone Pine, Buffalo Creek, Reno Lake, and Corral Creek, and the six-month timing adjustment, and hereby authorize you to implement these increases as follows:

Lone Pine	July 1	$1.30 per hour
	January 1	0.55 per hour
Buffalo Creek	September 1	1.30 per hour
	March 1	0.55 per hour
Reno Lake	November 1	1.30 per hour
	May 1	0.55 per hour
Corral Creek	July 1	12.1% average
		1.21 per hour
	January 1	0.60 per hour

Please keep me posted on the wage and economic conditions that occur between now and the implementation of the January 19—— increases.

Sincerely,

Conway Mining Company

John J. Mason
President

TO MANAGERS REGARDING SUMMARY FORMAT
FOR MAKING WAGE, BENEFITS,
AND WORK PRACTICES ANNOUNCEMENTS

  TO: All Department Managers

FROM: M. T. Grant

 SUBJ: WAGES, SUPPLEMENTAL BENEFITS, AND WORK PRACTICES FOR
        OPERATIONS EMPLOYEES

In order to ensure that all parties with a need to know are kept informed of hourly employee wage and benefits practices at our various locations, the attached summary format has been developed. This draft format, once finalized, will be used to document periodic changes in supplemental benefits and work practices which may impact recruiting, payroll, or labor relations policy. Wage rate sheets for each location are attached to this summary format.

Please review the summary with regard to completeness of the information needed by your department and return your comments to me by Friday, January 29, 19—— if you find that additional categories of information are needed.

PROPOSAL FOR IMPLEMENTING
A TRAVEL ALLOWANCE PROGRAM

  TO: L. G. Evanston, L. G. Waters, B. J. Carlton

FROM: L. Lambert

 SUBJ: VEHICLE MAINTENANCE ALLOWANCE (VMA) FOR
        WESTERN STATES COMPANY EMPLOYEES

Attached is the proposal, with initialed approvals, for implementing a travel allowance program for Western States Company employees.

Pursuant to these approvals, the program will be implemented on February 1, 19—— for first payments on the checks issued March 10. The approval for payment will be the responsibility of the General Manager, and will be transmitted to Payroll monthly with the Exception Report. The Exception Report will list the payment for each employee for that month. The VMA rate will be $4.50 per day.

VMA is taxable and will not be paid for vacation days, holidays, sick days, or days when the employee utilizes company transportation.

REVIEWING A VEHICLE MAINTENANCE ALLOWANCE
PROGRAM TO REPLACE VAN POOLS

Mr. Thomas V. Mann
Vice-President, Human Resources
Horn Manufacturing Company
One River Drive
Chicago, Illinois 60627

Dear Tom:

Due to the increase in size of the Lynwood Plant, it is no longer feasible to provide transportation to hourly employees in individual vehicles. A review of surrounding plants reflects the following policies:

Antelope Hills

Employees are paid for transportation, but subsidized bus service is provided at a cost equal to the travel allowance.

Red Butte

Employees are paid a per-diem allowance, determined by use of a Hertz national study on transportation costs. For 1983, Red Butte is recommending $5.10 per day (the calculation is attached).

Indian Bluffs

Vans are provided for transportation to the plant. An allowance is available for employees who cannot be serviced by vans and as a payment to the van driver. It also serves as a payment to employees when a van is not able to make its normal run.

For Lynwood, costs are estimated for providing either van service or a per-diem allowance. These are attached and show that at the $4.16-per-day allowance, the total per-day cost of $124.80 is a little more expensive than the estimated $123.04 cost for providing vans. Although less costly, this would seem to indicate that vans are the proper way to proceed and would be in keeping with our other operations. During start-up, personnel will be coming on randomly. If a van is provided then, it will be under-utilized and the cost per person will rise.

Since the vehicle maintenance allowance must be set in either case to provide driver payment, it is recommended that the allowance be established at $4.16 per day. Van service should be reviewed again in June when staffing conditions have stabilized. This will allow us to gauge reaction to the allowance. If we feel vans are still the most economical method of transportation we can move in that direction.

The allowance is a taxable addition to the employees' normal payroll. It is also intended that only one allowance be computed, based on Council Bluffs being the nearest full-service community.

In conclusion, practices at our other operations were reviewed. Costs were estimated for van-type transportation and individual allowances. Also checked was contract van service, which resulted in a $288.00-per-day cost. Van transportation appears slightly cheaper, but during initial operations could lose its cost effectiveness. It is recommended that $4.16 per day be established as the individual allowance effective on the February 5 payroll. Van operation will be reviewed later in the year to determine if a change should occur.

Sincerely,

Jeanne Moreau
Personnel Manager
Attachments

TRAVEL SUBSIDY

Based on Hertz National Driving Cost Study

Criteria:
Round trip miles to Council Bluffs	78 miles
National average employee travel to work	15 miles

Car pool of three individuals
Loan interest rate of 12.68%
Annual use: 25,000 miles
Vehicle used: Ford LTD II bought locally
 at 10% below list price
First year depreciation rate of 30%
Hertz 1980 costs inflated at 10% for 1981

List Price:	$9,200
Less 10%	920
	$8,280

Depreciation (30%)		$2,484
Fuel ($1.40/gal. @ 17 mi./gal.)		2,059
Insurance, License and Fees		1,216
(Ins: $777, License: $130, Tax: $309)		
Interest		1,049
Service:	0.0142/mi.—Hertz	355
Repair:	0.0332/mi.—Hertz	830
		$7,993

$7,993 ÷ 25,000 mi. = 0.3197/mi.

Red Cloud—round trip	78 mi.
Less—national average work travel	30
	48
Divide by three in car pool	÷ 3
	16 mi.

16 mi. × 0.3197 = $5.12 (use $5.10)

Total Annual Cost:

238 working days × 490 employees = 5.10 × 238 × 490 = $594,762

Current Annual Cost:

238 working days × 490 employees = 4.75 × 238 × 490 = 553,945

Difference:	$ 40,817
% Increase:	7.4%

TRAVEL COST ESTIMATES

Individual

Based on the attached Hertz study and Red Cloud computation

Vehicle operation	$0.3197/mi.
Prospect Point round trip	70 mi.
National average trip	−30 mi.
Allowance mileage	40 mi.

For three persons per car

    40 ÷ 3   =   13 mi.

    13 × \$0.3197   =   \$4.16 per day

Total cost per day

    30 personnel × \$4.16   =   \$124.80 per day

<u>Van Operating Cost</u>

From Antelope Hills

Gas	\$0.11
Maintenance	0.08
Lease	0.15
Insurance	0.03
License	<u>0.01</u>
	\$0.38 per mi.

Total cost per day—four vans @ 70 mi., four drivers @ \$4.16

    70 × 4 × \$0.38   =   \$106.40

    4 × \$4.16   =   <u>16.64</u>

                      \$123.04 per day

ANNOUNCING JOB DESCRIPTION REVIEW PROGRAM

    TO: A. V. Watson

FROM: L. A. Browne

  SUBJ: JOB DESCRIPTION REVIEW

As discussed at the recent Personnel Committee meeting, we will be conducting a review of all job evaluations in the range 850 to 1299 points over the next few months. In order to do this, it will be critically important to have up-to-date job descriptions for at least the specific benchmark positions by the end of February. All other positions in this point range should have updated job descriptions completed by the end of March.

Position	Job Description Review Date
Mgr. Devel. Services	
Mgr. Design Engineering	
Mgr. Project Engineering	
Mgr. Drafting, Graphics, & Reproduction	

We would appreciate it if you would contact the incumbents and ask them to prepare a draft of their accountabilities that reflects the responsibilities currently delegated to their positions.

I will be happy to work with them in finalizing job descriptions for your approval once drafts have been completed. I am attaching copies of descriptions currently held in our files, in order to facilitate the review process.

ANNOUNCING JOB EVALUATION COMMITTEE MEETING

TO: B. D. Douglas, D. J. Garno, T. A. Reid,
T. A. See, P. W. Green, J. A. Lincoln

FROM: G. H. Kuhnhausen

SUBJ: JOB EVALUATION COMMITTEE MEETING

The scheduled Job Evaluation Committee meeting date has been changed from July 6 to Tuesday, July 13, to accommodate prior commitments of some of the members.

Lunch will be served at 11:45 A.M. in Conference Room H. Please call Don Derks on extension 3022 to confirm your reservation for lunch. The meeting should conclude by 2:30 P.M.

TO VICE-PRESIDENT REGARDING NEW CAREER LADDERS

Mr. John W. Wilke
Vice-President
Environmental Services
Webster Company, Inc.
2027 Larimer Drive
Denver, Colorado 80203

Dear Mr. Wilke:

I am currently working on career ladders (promotional hierarchies) for several job families. Through discussions with Ralph Browne, we have identified the need for an environmental technician at a level higher than that of the currently approved technician position. We have also proposed the creation of an "entry level" technician, a position that would be non-degreed and require minimal experience.

This career ladder will provide growth opportunity for the incumbents as well as flexibility to the manager in identifying and selecting the appropriate working levels for subordinates. Tentative salary ranges for this group are:

Environmental Technician E/L	15.0–18.8
Environmental Technician	16.7–19.2
Sr. Environmental Technician	18.8–21.6
Environmental Specialist E/L	24.7–27.9

The description for the new senior level position is attached. This description was also developed working with Ralph Browne. The entry-level position description should be final prior to January, 19——.

Since the immediate use of these levels does not require an increase in the number of positions of the Environmental Services Department, an approval package is not necessary. Your approval, by signing this letter and returning it to me, will authorize the implementation of this hierarchy.

Sincerely,

Sarah L. Goldman
Manager of Compensation

TO VICE-PRESIDENT
REGARDING DECENTRALIZATION
OF PERSONNEL AND PAYROLL STAFF FUNCTIONS

Mr. Howard Steiner
Vice-President
Johnson-Steiner
6240 Frelner Street
Cheyenne, Wyoming 82006

Dear Howard:

In keeping with the Management Committee's decision to decentralize our staff functions, we are proceeding to transfer the hourly payroll for the Redwood facility from Denver to Cheyenne effective June 16, 19——. At that time, all relevant payroll records will be transferred. The records to be transferred include:

Each hourly employee's personal file (including those of terminated employees):

- Authorizations for pay rate changes
- Authorizations for deduction
- Record of vacation and sick days
- Copy of new hire form
- Original W-4

All year-to-date payroll information (including terminated employees):

- Employee name, Social Security number, employee I.D.
- Federal income tax withholding
- FICA deduction
- State income tax withholding
- FICA wages

Pertinent information relating to deductions:

- Thrift Plan
- GLIC
- United Fund
- Credit Union
- U.P. Stock Plan
- Savings Bonds
- Garnishments

The information, together with all files, will be delivered to the Redwood facility in June, and upon receipt of all records, Redwood personnel will create files according to the instructions in the Payroll Manual. The year-to-date information for each employee will be recorded on the new payroll system. The records will then be complete and available for the preparation of the first payroll to be distributed on July 2, 19—— and every other Thursday thereafter, with the exception of holidays.

The Denver Payroll Department will be responsible for the preparation of all second-quarter reports (FIT, FICA, Thrift Plan, etc.) and should retain copies of any records necessary for preparation of these reports. In addition, we will pay the hourly employees through June 15, 19——.

All payroll reports will be generated by Redwood and transmitted to the appropriate person or agency when due. The necessary reports are:

Payroll Reports	Due Date
Federal Income Tax	End of each pay period
FICA	End of each pay period
Federal Unemployment Tax	Quarterly
Wyoming Unemployment Tax	Quarterly
Wyoming Workers Compensation	Monthly
Thrift Plan	Monthly
Group Life Insurance Coverage	Monthly
Credit Union	End of each pay period
Savings Bonds	End of each pay period
Corporation Stock	As needed
Garnishments	As needed
Other Deductions	As needed
W-2s	January 31st

Payroll checks will be signed by T. L. Fry, general manager of the Redwood facility.

We will be available during the week of June 16th to assist with the transfer. Please call me as soon as you've had an opportunity to read this letter. We can discuss any problems you foresee, in order to ensure a smooth payroll transition.

Sincerely,

Loren Haley
Director of Human Resources

PROVIDING LIST OF COMPLETED PERFORMANCE APPRAISALS

Mr. Glen E. Johnson
Vice-President, Human Resources
Tomac Medical Components Corporation
16000 Greenwood Plaza
Denver, Colorado 80211

Dear Mr. Johnson:

Pursuant to your request, we have checked our records and they indicate that as of June 1, 19——, Performance Appraisals have not been completed for the employees listed below. Reminders were sent to the responsible managers regarding the late appraisals. An asterisk indicates that no appraisal was received in either 19—— or 19——.

	Employee	Manager
January 19——:	L. Mackey*	J. Browne
	J. Hynes	J. Browne
	F. Hayes	C. Corning
February 19——:	R. Seton*	J. Browne
March 19——:	F. Peel	C. Corning
	D. Lang	M. Mason
	A. Gomez	M. Mason
April 19——:	M. Ryan*	L. Yates
	F. Frank	C. Corning

Please advise what action you would like us to take.

Sincerely,

Jean M. Lincoln
Compensation Manager

PROVIDING FOLLOW-UP PROCEDURES FOR COMPLETION OF PERFORMANCE APPRAISALS

       TO: All Managers
     FROM: R. T. Greene
     SUBJ: 19—— PERFORMANCE APPRAISALS

In 19——, approximately 510 employees should have received performance appraisals. Thirty are currently delinquent. Our follow-up procedure this year has been to:

1. Send a reminder to the manager approximately 30 days prior to the due date and another reminder, with a copy to his superior, one month later.
2. Send a periodic report to the appropriate vice-president identifying all late appraisals.
3. Discuss overdue appraisals with the Management Committee.

Several of the performance appraisals were not given due to extenuating circumstances, and these are identified.

We will continue to monitor the performance appraisal process and hope that several of the delinquent reports may still be submitted.

PROVIDING INFORMATION
ON ANNUALIZED TURNOVER

Mr. Thomas M. Jones
Director,
Compensation Planning
Tidewater Corporation
500 Park Avenue
New York, New York 10154

Dear Tom:

Pursuant to our telephone conversation, I have attached a computer list of exempt employees who have terminated during 19——. During this time, our average population for this group has been 264. The annualized turnover through the end of June was $23-264 \times 2=17.4$ percent; the rate in 19—— was 12.5 percent.

Please advise me if you require additional data.

Sincerely,

Lauren M. Keys
Manager, Compensation

3

Letters Regarding Benefits, Insurance Claims, Vacations, and Holidays

This is a very specialized field because of the many laws that govern administration of benefits. The personnel manager must either have a good background in the field or must call on benefits experts to provide the needed expertise in correspondence. A Prentice-Hall publication recently reported that benefits have now exceeded $6,600 per employee, so it's important to communicate well in this expensive personnel area.

Even if you know all areas of the benefits field, including proper administration, you must be able to communicate the various programs to top management and to employees, and it takes a different style for each group. Top executives are interested in facts, reasons why, total costs, administrative details, and budgets. Employees are interested in amounts of individual coverage, time needed for claims resolution, how to claim benefits, and so forth. Correspondence to either group should address the needs of that particular group. After you have written a letter to employees about benefits, give it to an employee to read before you mail it out. Ask the employee if he understands the memo. If he can't tell you what it says, start over.

MANAGER'S TIPS ON BENEFITS CORRESPONDENCE

- When writing to employees about their benefits and clarifying coverage, keep it simple but go into enough detail that they thoroughly understand what you've said. Use short sentences, simple words, and paragraphs that don't run on—maybe four or five sentences to a paragraph, depending on the situation.

• One of the best ways to communicate benefits to employees is with a question-and-answer section.

Example

Q: How do I file a medical claim?

A: Pick up a blank claim form in the Personnel Department, complete the section marked "For Employee," take it to your doctor and have the doctor complete the section marked "For Physician." Return the completed, signed form to the Personnel Department for processing.

• Benefit letters should communicate the following things immediately:

1. Technical expertise
2. Clarifying
3. Caring
4. Timeliness

**TO EMPLOYEES COVERING
ANNUAL REPORT
OF EMPLOYEE BENEFIT PLANS**

Dear Fellow Employees:

As a Crossland Electronics employee, you participate in many excellent benefit plans. If you or a member of your family incurred medical expenses this past year, you are certainly aware of the value of the Medical Insurance Plan. If you have started to plan for your future financial security, you know the importance of the Pension and Thrift plans.

Chances are you are not aware of the extent of the company's cost for providing these benefits. For this reason, we are mailing under separate cover a Summary Annual Report of Employee Benefit Plans for 19———. The report is an annual statement on the financial management of certain benefits—those that are insured or have assets in the Trust Fund. In it you will find facts and figures on the following plans:

- Pension
- Life Insurance
- Medical
- Business Travel
  Accident Insurance
- Employee Stock Ownership
- Savings
- Dental
- Accidental Death and
  Dismemberment Insurance

When you consider the vital protection these plans provide, it is easy to see the importance of maintaining them on a financially sound basis. As the report shows, we can be confident that our benefits will be there when we need them. The company pays the entire cost for all these plans, except for any contributions you may make to the Savings Plan and Employee Stock Ownership Plan.

Important as these plans are, they form only part of the total benefit package. For example, you are also eligible for sick pay, long-term disability, and educational assistance. Another benefit—your yearly vacation entitlement—grows automatically with your career at Crossland.

If you have any questions on this report or any other aspect of your employee benefit program, please contact Lane K. Blake, manager, Compensation and Benefits.

Sincerely,

Larry W. Wisner
Vice-President
Human Resources

TO EMPLOYEES OUTLINING
IMPROVEMENTS IN PENSION PLAN

Dear Fellow Employees:

I am pleased to inform you of significant improvements in the Crossland Electronics Pension Plan.

As you may know, your pension benefits are determined by considering three factors:

- Your years of credited service
- The amount of your final average earnings, and
- The amount of your primary Social Security benefit.

These three factors are used in the benefit formula that determines the pension benefit you will be entitled to receive at retirement.

The plan improvements, which are effective as of October 1, 19——, include the following:

- Final Average Earnings (FAE) will now be based on the highest 36 consecutive months out of the last 120 months. Previously, FAE was based on the highest 60 consecutive months out of the last 120 months.

- The offset of Social Security and other primary government benefits will now be determined by taking 1.375 percent for each year of credited service up to 40 years. A flat offset of 55 percent was formerly used to calculate benefits.

- A minimum pension has been established that will guarantee you a benefit of $150 for each year of credited service you have had with the company, provided you have at least 10 years of credited service. This amount would be payable should your pension calculation yield a benefit less than this minimum amount.

We are confident these fine improvements will enhance the financial security of you and your family upon your retirement. In the near future, you will receive a revised Retirement section for your Employee Benefit Handbook explaining the improved plan in more detail. In the meantime, if you have any questions concerning the pension plan, please contact the Human Resources Department.

Sincerely,

Larry W. Wisner
Vice-President
Human Resources

LETTER TO EMPLOYEES
ANNOUNCING A NEW BENEFIT

MEMO TO: All Employees
      SUBJ: Vision Care Insurance

We are pleased to announce that Las Vegas Delivery Company has approved an additional benefit for permanent full-time employees.

Commencing July 1st, vision care insurance will be provided to employees who have completed six months of full-time employment with the Company.

Employees who wish to participate in this new benefit program should obtain an enrollment card from the Personnel Department, complete the card, and forward it to the Payroll Department during the first week in July. When you pick up the enrollment card you will receive a brochure that provides details of the vision care benefits. A personnel representative will also be available to answer your questions.

This new benefit is an expression of concern for the health of our employees and their families and we hope that you will take advantage of it in the coming months.

TO AN EMPLOYEE REGARDING BENEFITS
AFTER SIX MONTHS OF SERVICE

Mr. James L. Lewis
4360 Nineteenth Street
Denver, Colorado 80215

Dear Jim:

The Company's Employee Benefit Program has been designed to provide benefits for employees who meet certain service requirements. Now that you are approaching six months of service with us, you will soon be eligible for the following benefits:

Dental Insurance Plan

You will become eligible for dental coverage on October 1, 19——.

The Dental Plan, which is paid entirely by the Company, is designed to pay a significant portion of the dental expenses incurred by you and your family. Some of the main features of the plan are:

- Diagnostic and preventive services: Paid at 100 percent of reasonable and customary charges.
- Basic and restorative services: Paid at 80 percent of reasonable and customary charges, after satisfying a $50 deductible for each covered person once each calendar year.
- Prosthetic services (bridgework, crowns, dentures): Payable at 50 percent of reasonable and customary charges.

- The total amount payable for the foregoing services in any one calendar year is $750 per person.
- Orthodontic benefits: Not subject to the $50 deductible or the annual maximum of $750. The plan will pay 50 percent of the orthodontist's charges up to a lifetime maximum of $650 for dependents to age 19.

The level of coverage under the plan is excellent, but please note that important time requirements must be met to receive the maximum payment.

COVERAGE BECOMES EFFECTIVE ON THE FIRST DAY OF THE MONTH FOLLOWING COMPLETION OF SIX MONTHS OF SERVICE. Charges incurred before this date will not be covered.

At least SIX MONTHS must elapse between routine check-ups and cleanings in order for the work to be covered at 100 percent of the reasonable and customary charges. A deviation of only one day will result in a denial of coverage. Please monitor carefully the timing of the visits.

Full-mouth X rays are covered in full under the terms of the policy only once every THREE YEARS.

Attached for your reference and future use is a Dental Claim Form. Read the instructions and be sure to follow them carefully when you submit a claim for benefits. Pay special attention to the first set of instructions regarding the Predetermination Procedure when charges will exceed $100.00.

Salary Continuation Plan

If you should become ill or injured and unable to work for a period of time, Salary Continuation benefits help replace your regular income. This important financial protection is fully paid for by the Company.

This benefit, based on your earnings and length of service, ranges from two weeks of pay at 100 percent of base salary after six months of service to 18 weeks at 100 percent plus an additional eight weeks at 75 percent of base salary after 10 years or more of service.

Benefits are payable starting with the first day of disability and will continue in accordance with the schedule on Page D-1 of your Benefit Handbook.

Educational Assistance Program

The Company encourages continuing educational development through a generous Educational Assistance Program. This program offers you 100 percent reimbursement for any approved, work-related course that you complete successfully or that the Company has requested that you take.

This is only a brief description of your benefits. For further details of these plans, you may refer to the Employee Benefit Handbook which was given to you at the time you were employed.

Sincerely,

Lois C. Bowman
Benefits Manager

TO EMPLOYEE TELLING
HOW TO FILE A CLAIM FOR BENEFITS

Ms. Mary Lowell
Post Office Box 370
Rock Springs, Wyoming 82942

Dear Ms. Lowell:

It is easy for you to file a medical claim under the Company's Benefit Plan.

- First—Your claim must be for a covered medical expense.
- Second—You must file a separate claim form for each covered individual.
- Third—You must complete a separate claim form each time a claim is filed.

For each claim filed, you are required to:

1. Complete Items 1–5 on the claim form.
2. Sign your name on Item 5.
3. Give the claim form to your physician or provider of service to complete his portion of the form.

OR

Submit itemized *original* bills.

- Physician's statement must provide a diagnosis and a complete description and breakdown of charges that are included, along with a signature and I.D. number.
- Drug bills must contain the patient's name, physician's name, prescription number, date filed, and amount.

4. Return the completed claim form with attachments, if any, to:

Employee Benefits Department
Rocky Mountain Oil & Gas
777 – 17th Street
Denver, CO 80202

You may wish to retain a copy of the claim form, with attachments, for your personal records before filing the claim with us. After we certify and log the claim, it will be submitted to Equitable for processing.

Upon processing of the claim, Equitable will pay benefits directly to you or the physician or provider of services as indicated on the claim form. A fully detailed explanation of benefits will be provided to you each time a claim is processed; we will also receive a copy.

Should you have any questions or problems regarding your claim, please contact us, and if necessary, we will work with Equitable on your behalf.

Sincerely,

Richard M. Dirkson
Manager
Compensation and Benefits

TO BENEFITS CARRIER REGARDING
DENIAL OF CERTAIN CLAIMS

Mr. Lewis Wilson
Benefits Director
Tilden Corporation
300 Lake Front Drive
Chicago, Illinois 60616

Dear Lew:

On numerous occasions since the dental plan became effective, we have had employees who for various reasons (some cosmetic, some not) have had orthodontia treatment. In many of these instances, the employees were single, with no dependents. Some find it hard to understand why other employees' children are covered for the same type of treatment while they are not. They feel the plan discriminates against single people or married people with no children.

The total cost per year for an employee covered for the maximum benefit of $650 is about $325, since the payments are normally spread over two years. The employee still bears a considerable share of the cost and usually does not commit to the treatment unless he or she feels strongly that it is necessary.

The age-19 restriction was realistic until a few years ago, when adults began to wear braces for the same reasons that children do. We recommend the restriction be reviewed with the intention of removing it from the dental program.

Please give me your thoughts on the subject. I will be in Chicago on June 14, and will come by your office to discuss it further.

Sincerely,

Mary Mahoney
District Manager
Employee Benefits

HEALTH MAINTENANCE ORGANIZATION (HMO)
ACTIVATION LETTER

Mr. William W. Brooks
Benefits Manager, Western District
Longmont Manufacturing Company
One Technical Center
Longmont, Colorado 80502

Dear Bill:

As you know, the Kaiser Foundation Health Plan, a federally qualified HMO, contacted Longmont Manufacturing Company earlier this year with the intent of enrolling current employees in their HMO program.

Upon reviewing the Kaiser program, we noticed the large difference between the Kaiser and current Longmont premium rates. We notified Kaiser of the difference, anticipating that Kaiser would not actively pursue an activation under the HMO Act. However, Kaiser has informed us that they wish to proceed with a formal activation and enrollment of employees, regardless of the difference in rates.

We have therefore tentatively scheduled a meeting with Mrs. Jean White, an enrollment representative of Kaiser, for November 15 at 11:00 A.M. at the Kaiser office in Lakewood. At this meeting, we will have an opportunity to tour the Kaiser facilities, as well as go over timetables and procedures that will allow you ample time to offer the Kaiser option. We would like to meet with you at your office at 9:00 A.M. on November 15, before the Kaiser meeting.

Please advise if this schedule is convenient.

Sincerely,

Joseph A. Gardino
Corporate Benefits Director

REVIEWING COMPANY POLICY ON SALARY INCREASES WHEN EMPLOYEE IS ON LEAVE OF ABSENCE

Mr. Robert van Dorn
14310 Ralston Road
Arvada, Colorado 80006

Dear Bob:

In response to our phone conversation yesterday, I am setting out the company policy regarding salary increases effective while an employee is on leave of absence.

The Disability Policy defines earnings as "...your regular rate of monthly compensation, excluding bonuses and overtime, in effect immediately before your disability begins." If a salary increase is processed to become effective during a period of paid disability, your salary continuation of LTD benefits will not be affected.

Benefit levels for life insurance, vacations, and pension will be increased on the effective date of the salary change. Thrift Plan is not affected since it is a function of pay actually received by an employee.

Please advise me if you have questions about the policy. I hope you are on the road to recovery and will be able to return to work soon.

Sincerely,

Joseph A. Gardino
Corporate Benefits Director

LONG-TERM DISABILITY BENEFITS
IN THE EVENT OF LAYOFF OR TERMINATION

Mr. Larry M. Hanson
Manager, Compensation & Benefits
Union Off-Shore Oil Corporation
9229 Sunset Boulevard
Los Angeles, California 90069

    Re: Long-Term Disability Benefits

Dear Larry:

In reference to your letter concerning the treatment of employees who have partial, temporary, or permanent disabilities in the event of a layoff/termination situation, please be advised that these employees should be treated in the same manner as any other employees under present policy, as follows:

- An employee who is physically able to perform the functions of the assigned position would receive the same severance benefits as any other employee, based on service and salary.
- An employee who is temporarily disabled may qualify for the Salary Continuation Plan. After the employee is no longer eligible for Salary Continuation benefits, either due to recovery or exhaustion of benefits, the employee would be treated in the same manner as any other severanced employee, unless the employee then qualifies for the Long-Term Disability Plan (LTD).
- An employee who qualifies for LTD (i.e., six months or more of active service, exhaustion of Salary Continuation Plan payments, or is "Totally Disabled" [LTD definition]), would be placed on LTD and receive LTD benefits in accordance with the Plan provisions.

Proof of disability for Salary Continuation can be an appropriate statement from the employee's physician. If it is felt that additional information or verification of disability is necessary, the employee may be sent to a doctor or clinic selected by the company. In either case, the physician or clinic should be provided with details of the employee's responsibilities and requested to indicate which duties can or cannot be performed due to the disability. This information is extremely valuable to the employee and the company since it may enable us to alter the position responsibilities to accommodate the disability or assist in the rehabilitation.

Proof of total disability for Long-Term Disability benefits is the same as previously outlined; however, the option of a company-selected physician or clinic confirming that the employee is "totally disabled" is a minimum requirement of the Named Fiduciary-Plan Administration of the Wymore Corporation Long-Term Disability Plan. Additionally, the Named Fiduciary-Plan Administration may require that the employee qualify for disability benefit payments from Social Security.

Attached for your use is an outline of the recommended administrative procedures to be followed under the Salary Continuation and Long-Term Disability Plans. If you have any additional questions, please call me.

Sincerely,

Lawrence T. Smith
Vice-President
Employee Benefits

TO EMPLOYEE REGARDING BENEFITS
UPON TERMINATION

Ms. Martha Bolling
3742 Sherman Street
Denver, Colorado 80202

Dear Ms. Bolling:

We regret the need to reduce our staff and want to be sure that you are aware of several important items regarding your benefit programs.

The Medical and Life Insurance policies contain provisions that may allow an employee to convert the group insurance to an individual policy, provided that certain provisions are met. If you are interested in exercising one or both of these options, it is important that you contact the Employee Relations Department as soon as possible.

Employees who have contributed to the Thrift Plan must complete a Form TP-5 to withdraw contributions. This form must be completed even if you have withdrawn your funds previously. It takes approximately six weeks from the end of the month in which the form is received to process the distribution.

If, based on age and years of service, you are eligible for a vested pension benefit, you will receive a vesting certificate specifying the amount of earned pension.

If we can be of further service to you, please do not hesitate to call me.

Sincerely,

Paul Doulent
Benefits Manager

TO EMPLOYEE REGARDING BENEFITS CONVERSION

Mr. John C. Adams
10136 20th Street
Apt. 402
Lakewood, Colorado 80215

Dear John:

I understand you will be terminating your employment at the end of October to continue your education. This memo is to advise you of the status of three key benefits.

Pension

By terminating prior to achieving your ten-year anniversary date, you will forfeit all interest in the company pension plan.

Thrift Plan

You have never participated in the Thrift Plan; therefore, no benefit status is applicable.

You will have the opportunity to convert your medical and life insurance to individual policies. It may be to your advantage, however, to explore the coverage offered by your school, because they tend to provide acceptable coverage at a lower premium than our insurance company offers.

Sincerely,

Richard W. Browne
Benefits Coordinator

TO INSURANCE CARRIER AMENDING
BENEFITS AT TERMINATION

Mr. Frank L. Weatherly
The Equitable Life Assurance Society
   of the United States
810 Seventh Avenue, Suite 2600
New York, New York 10019

>   Re: Medical Insurance Plan IV
>   Policy No. 67320

Dear Mr. Weatherly:

Please amend our Medical Insurance Plan IV to provide for extended benefits for an employee, if such employee has been terminated from active employment as a result of a layoff from the company, for up to a period of 60 days.

At the end of this 60-day period, the employee's insurance will end unless he or she returns to active employment.

If you have any questions, please give me a call.

Sincerely,

Lloyd K. Deere
Benefits Administrator

TO DIVISION PERSONNEL MANAGER SENDING A SUPPLY OF SUMMARY ANNUAL REPORTS—ERISA

Mr. Don L. Meyers
Director, Employee Relations
Denver Division
Wymore Corporation
One Energy Center
Denver, Colorado 80202

Dear Don:

Enclosed please find a supply of the Summary Annual Report of Employee Benefit Plans for distribution to every Plan participant.

This package contains 500 reports that are to be distributed to all employees of Wymore Corporation.

Distribution of these reports is to be made by November 15 and must be in accordance with the Department of Labor regulations. The general rule is that the Summary Annual Report must be mailed to participants by first class mail. Alternative methods, such as hand or personal delivery, are also acceptable, as long as they are reasonably calculated to ensure delivery.

Should you have any additional questions, please call me.

Sincerely,

William M. Haland
Vice-President
Compensation and Benefits

ERISA LETTER TO PENSION PLAN ADMINISTRATOR

Mr. Adam T. Grant
7359 Ivy Lane
Littleton, Colorado 80121

Dear Mr. Grant:

ERISA requires the Pension Plan Administrator to provide each Plan participant and beneficiary with a summary of the Annual Report filed with the Internal Revenue Service each year.

Attached you will find a Summary Annual Report for the Plan Year 19——. This report will inform you of the financial status of the Plans and also help to provide an understanding of the costs required to maintain this valuable benefit.

If you should have any questions concerning the content of this report, please contact Laurence L. Lighter, Compensation and Benefits, Portland Management Group, 503 Mason Street, Portland, Oregon 97222.

Sincerely,

R. F. Stevens
Named Fiduciary-Plan
Administration Representative

CONFIRMATION OF MEETING ON EMPLOYEE BENEFITS STATEMENT

Mr. Larry M. Hanson
Manager, Compensation & Benefits
Union Off-Shore Oil Corporation
9229 Sunset Boulevard
Los Angeles, California 90069

Dear Larry:

This will confirm the organizational meeting for the 19—— Employee Benefit Statement to be held October 8, 19—— at 9:00 A.M. at our Headquarters in Los Angeles. At this meeting, we will review:

- revisions and additions to the content of the Benefit Statement,
- areas of responsibilities for operating companies, and
- coordination and timing of activities.

The meeting should also help to coordinate the Thrift Plan Normal Distribution for 19——.

It will be necessary to have you and the appropriate Accounting and Information Systems personnel in attendance.

In order to help you prepare for October 8th, we have enclosed an agenda and schedules for the Thrift Plan and Benefit Statement. Please give me a call if you have any questions.

Sincerely,

Lawrence T. Smith
Vice-President
Employee Benefits

TO EMPLOYEE REGARDING
BENEFITS AFTER AGE 65

Ms. Laura M. Watson
1530 Crabapple Road
Golden, Colorado 80401

Dear Ms. Watson:

Since you have elected to continue employment with Portland Management Group past age 65, please be advised that a post-65 benefit program has been developed and is now in operation. It is as follows:

Pension Plan

- Limit accrual of pension credit, earnings, and Social Security offset to age 65.
- No pension will be payable until the Postponed Retirement date.
- Surviving spouse's pension, equal to 50 percent of the pension payable to you during retirement, is in effect provided you were married for at least 12 months.

Life Insurance

- Reduce life insurance to one times annual salary at age 65. This coverage is paid in full by the company. Upon retirement, your coverage will remain the same, provided you contribute $1.70 per month per $1,000 of coverage (maximum contribution: $34.00 per month).

Long-Term Disability

- Continue eligibility and benefit payments until age 65 when you would be eligible for normal retirement under the Pension Plan.
- If you become disabled after age 60, disability income will continue for five years, or to recovery, or to age 70, whichever comes first. At age 65, however, the amount you would be eligible to receive from the Pension Plan would be offset against your Long-Term Disability benefits.

Medical Plan

- Coordinate the Medical Plan with Medicare. This means our plan would pay up to the amount not paid by Medicare. We would also reimburse you $10 per month to cover the cost of Medicare Part B (Medical). At retirement, you may contribute to the Retiree Medical Plan. Your contributions will depend upon your dependents' ages. You will also assume the full cost of Medicare Part B.

For the following plans, continue present coverage until retirement:

Thrift Plan
Dental
Accidental Death & Dismemberment
Business Travel Accident
Salary Continuation

If you have any questions about this program, please do not hesitate to contact your benefits representative.

Sincerely,

Ralph A. Cox
Benefits Manager

REQUEST FOR PENSION VESTING CERTIFICATE TO BE SENT TO RETIRING EMPLOYEE

Mr. Lewis Wilson
Benefits Director
Tilden Corporation
300 Lake Front Drive
Chicago, Illinois 60616

Dear Lewis:

Please have a pension vesting certificate prepared for Harold Brown, who was terminated on September 14, 19———. Harold was originally hired on March 16, 19———. His pensionable earnings for the last 12 years are listed below:

19———	$19,824	19———	$25,925
19———	18,321	19———	28,130
19———	17,820	19———	32,450
19———	19,378	19———	35,672
19———	21,525	19———	39,421
19———	22,925	19———	32,501 (to date)

If you have any questions or need more information, please call me.

Sincerely,

Mary Mahoney
District Manager
Employee Benefits

REQUEST FOR FORMS NECESSARY
TO PAY DEATH BENEFITS

Mr. Ned Snyder
General Manager
Wymore Corporation
Post Office Box 607
Cheyenne, Wyoming 82001

Dear Ned:

I have enclosed the forms that Lena Doe should complete in order to obtain her husband's Group Life and Accidental Death benefits. The AD&D form also requires statements from the attending physician and the mortician. You should complete the Employer's Statement.

Once the forms are complete, return them to me along with two certified copies of the Death Certificate.

Please extend our sympathies to Mrs. Doe, and assure her that we are available to assist her in any way possible.

Sincerely,

Linda Johnson
Manager
Compensation and Benefits

LETTER QUESTIONING CLAIMS PROCESSING TIME

Mr. Mark J. Torres
Assistant Benefits Manager
The General Life Assurance Company
  of America
136 Jones Street
Kansas City, Kansas 66205

Dear Mr. Torres:

I am enclosing a letter and claims log from Mrs. Jean Thompson at Electronic Data Services Corporation concerning General's claims turnaround time and unresolved claims.

We have selected a small sample of claims on the log for you to measure actual turnaround time. Please prepare a report showing date received, date paid, and number of work days required for processing.

As of May 19—— we have resolved our problems with turnaround time since your last five weekly claim reports indicate that 80 percent of the claims are processed within five work days, with the remaining 20 percent of the claims processed within another one to five days. Mrs. Thompson indicates a nine-work-day average for April, with a six-and-one-half-work-day average at month's end. These figures are consistent with the significant improvement in turnaround time we experienced during April 19——.

Additionally, Mrs. Thompson indicates on the log that there are a number of claims for which no response has been received from General. Please review these claims and indicate their status to me.

In the future, we will follow up with General on any "no response" claims within 12 work days from date mailed. If this is acceptable to you, please advise me accordingly.

If you require any further information, please let me know.

Sincerely,

Harold T. Bradford
Manager, Employee Benefits

REGARDING DECENTRALIZATION OF BENEFITS ADMINISTRATION

Mr. Richard J. Jones
Post Office Box 27561
Los Angeles, California 90069

Dear Dick:

Our corporate meeting on the decentralization of the Life Insurance Plan administration to the Operating Companies is scheduled for September 9, 19——, 9:00 A.M., at corporate headquarters in Chicago, Illinois.

We will review administrative procedures for Life Insurance, Management Information System (MIS) needs for calculation of income, and the transfer of individual Life Insurance records. In addition to your Employee Benefits staff, we would suggest that a technical representative be present from your Management Information Services group.

Should you have any other questions or concerns, they can be presented at the meeting.

Sincerely,

Gilbert W. Johnson
Vice-President
Compensaton and Benefits

IMPLEMENTATION OF
DIRECT CLAIMS ADMINISTRATION

Mr. Richard M. Dirkson
Manager, Compensation and Benefits
Rocky Mountain Oil & Gas Company
717 – 17th Street
Denver, Colorado 80202

Dear Dick:

At our meeting of September 9, 19——, we reviewed the feasibility of a switchover to Direct Claims Administration (DCA) from the current employer-certified claims administration, and concluded that it should be implemented effective April 1, 19——.

To provide an orderly transition and ensure a continuity of service, the following tasks must be accomplished by March 15, 19——:

- Development of Management Information System (MIS) interface with Equitable's Group Eligibility Maintenance System (GEM) according to record format specifications.
- Listing and translation of all records of eligible employees, widows, retirees, and dependents onto GEM record formats on magnetic tape for initial submission to Equitable.
- List of Employee Relations and MIS staff representatives responsible for maintenance of internal DCA data base and monthly update of additions and deletions via magnetic tape switch.
- Preparation of DCA claim kits that include envelopes, revised claim forms, and return address envelopes to replace existing claim forms.
- Preparation of employee communication on DCA switchover to include announcement letter, claims kit, revised pages for medical section of Benefit Handbook, and an outline of the new administrative procedures.
- Preparation of internal administrative procedures for operating company use.
- Distribution of communication package and supply of claims kits to operating companies for release to employees.

Representatives from your Employee Relations and MIS Departments were provided with the information required to complete the switchover to DCA. If they have any outstanding technical questions, they should contact Mr. Jose R. Montalvo for resolution. Upon their completion of the first three tasks listed above, please notify us immediately. We will perform the next four tasks and establish the administrative liaison with Equitable.

Direct Claims Administration should improve turnaround time, enhance confidentiality, and provide other positive side effects, such as monitoring of dependent eligibility and gathering of census data. Employee Relations' involvement with employees on claims administration should continue for inquiries and problems.

Should you have any questions, please contact me.

Sincerely,

Lloyd L. Bennett
Vice-President
Compensation and Benefits

THANK YOU FOR ASSISTANCE IN ESTABLISHING BENEFITS FOR A NEW ORGANIZATION

Ms. Jean Black
City National Bank
Boulder, Colorado 80302

Dear Jean:

I am writing to thank you for the assistance and consideration you extended to Tom Carter and me in our efforts to establish an Employee Benefit Program for the Boulder Computer Services Group. The information you provided has been invaluable, and we appreciate the time you took from your busy schedule to talk with us.

If we can ever be of assistance to you, please don't hesitate to call. Again, thank you. It was a pleasure meeting you.

Yours very truly,

Gene Rolfsmeyer
Manager, Employee Benefits

REGARDING SALARY CONTINUATION FOR AN ILL EMPLOYEE

Daniel S. Goldman
Rocky Mountain Multiple Sclerosis Center
P.O. Box L283
Denver, Colorado 80262

Dear Mr. Goldman:

One of our employees, Ruth K. Johnson, is a recent patient of the Multiple Sclerosis Center. Our company's policy is to be supportive when an employee becomes disabled, and it is our intention, with your support, to work with Ruth to develop a flexible work schedule that will accommodate both her and the company. Our salary continuation program will pay her for time missed.

For our records, we need documentation regarding Ruth's condition and what might be expected in the way of impairment. I have drafted a letter that contains the main points that should be addressed.

A letter from your office would be appreciated. We are hopeful that there will be no deterioration of her condition, but if there is, I would welcome the opportunity to meet with you so we might develop a program that will allow her to continue working as long as possible.

Thank you for your consideration.

Sincerely,

Robert L. Rasmussen
Employee Benefits

BENEFITS FOR PART-TIME EMPLOYEES

TO: All Permanent Part-Time Employees

FROM: Colleen Haley, Director, Human Resources

SUBJ: BENEFITS FOR PERMANENT PART-TIME EMPLOYEES

We have had some questions recently from permanent part-time employees regarding their benefit programs. The following paragraph is taken from our Personnel Policy Manual.

Individuals hired as permanent part-time employees who work at least 20 hours a week for more than five months a year will be eligible for Life and Medical Insurance from date of hire, and Dental Insurance on the first of the month following one year of service.

Please call me if you need additional information.

REGARDING YEARLY HOLIDAY SCHEDULE

TO: All Employees

FROM: Mary F. Cook
Director, Employee Relations

SUBJ: 19—— HOLIDAY SCHEDULE

During 19——, the Company will provide the following 10 paid holidays for employees:

February 21	Monday	President's Day
April 1	Friday	Good Friday
May 30	Monday	Memorial Day
July 1	Friday	Floating Holiday
July 4	Monday	Independence Day
September 5	Monday	Labor Day
November 24	Thursday	Thanksgiving Day
November 25	Friday	Thanksgiving Friday
December 23	Friday	Christmas Holiday
December 26	Monday	Floating Holiday

4

Letters Concerning Human Resource Development Programs, Training Programs, and Consultant Services

Training information is best communicated in first-person telling or sharing style. The recipients of correspondence about training want to learn something from you, and so expect the message to be informative, brief, and to the point.

MANAGER'S TIPS ON TRAINING CORRESPONDENCE

- The manager has to sell programs to management and to employees, so a sales approach can work if it's not a "hard-sell" or a self-serving approach.

- Personnel and training people feel so strongly about the importance of training they sometimes make the mistake of promoting their programs on an emotional rather than a purely business level. This is a mistake. People have a short attention span for programs they perceive are being pushed on them.

- Training people have to be careful also not to get caught up in the "buzz word" syndrome in their writing and talking—HRD, CRT, CBT, and so on. Buzz words turn people off when they aren't part of that industry.

- As a training manager, you are expected to be a good communicator and are frequently judged by the effectiveness of your written and verbal communications skills as much as by your ability to develop and present training programs. Letters are evidence of your communications ability.

REGARDING USE OF EDUCATIONAL TAPE PROGRAM

TO: All Supervisors and Managers

FROM: Mary F. Cook

SUBJ: ASI EDUCATIONAL TAPES

The ASI educational tape for July is "Listen, Please."

Upon completion of this tape, participants will:

- Understand the need and importance of careful listening; and
- Know how to evaluate communication effectiveness according to proficiency in listening.

This course will be especially helpful to those who interview and conduct performance appraisals.

Please circulate this memo in your department. Interested employees can contact Mary Wood, ext. 326, by July 10th. The schedule for the 30-minute tape will be established once employee interest is determined.

LETTERS ON IN-HOUSE AND OUTSIDE TRAINING PROGRAMS: SAMPLE ONE

TO: All Managers

FROM: Elliott Payne

SUBJ: MANAGEMENT DEVELOPMENT OPPORTUNITY

A MANAGEMENT DEVELOPMENT COURSE FOR MANAGERS

Beginning October 14th, the Xerox Learning course, Management Communication Skills, will be presented in-house.

This nationally acclaimed program, recently purchased, focuses on the management function of directing. It is based on the premise that improvements in performance and productivity will result from the ability of managers to promote and sustain better communication and motivation on the part of subordinates.

Sounds great, right? Like me, you probably see such statements on classic motivation theory on literally dozens of management seminar brochures every day. So, how is this management course different?

Xerox Learning has gone one step further in program design. Unlike most management courses/seminars I've participated in, Xerox has taken classic motivation theory and built a course that teaches skills rather than imparts theory alone. Formal lecture is minimal in this course, with your active participation maximized throughout.

The program will be conducted for two and one-half days, October 14 and 15, 8:30 A.M. to 3:30 P.M., and October 16, 8:00 A.M. to noon.

The class is limited to 10 participants, on a first-come, first-served basis. Contact me on extension 2903 for your reservation.

LETTERS ON IN-HOUSE AND OUTSIDE
TRAINING PROGRAMS: SAMPLE TWO

TO: All RME Managers and Supervisors
FROM: E. E. Payne
SUBJ: DEVELOPMENTAL PROGRAM FOR SUPPORT STAFF

A half-day program, entitled "Management Education for Support Staff," has been scheduled for Monday, April 11th, from 8:30 A.M. to noon. The program is designed to be a developmental session for non-exempt employees, including those in the secretarial, clerical, and technical levels. Through this program, I believe your support staff will be able to make even greater contributions to the objectives of your department.

Participants will learn many helpful ideas about human relations, teamwork, motivation, and personal organization. James E. Allen, who is an experienced manager, a seasoned consultant to top management, and a skillful presenter, will conduct the program. I can personally recommend Mr. Allen as one of the best presenters on these topics in the field today.

A general announcement with registration information will be forthcoming. Prior supervisory approval is required for attendance. Each department will be responsible for providing for its own necessary telephone coverage while the program is in session.

If you have questions, please call me on ext. 2913.

LETTERS ON IN-HOUSE AND OUTSIDE
TRAINING PROGRAMS: SAMPLE THREE

Mr. Tony Narducci
Xerox Learning Systems
450 West Algonquin Road
Arlington Heights, Illinois 60005

Dear Tony:

According to Susan Cowal of your Denver staff, you are to be our session leader for "Interpersonal Managing Skills," January 21–23, 19——.

The program will be conducted at our new Corporate Headquarters, about 10 miles northwest of downtown Denver (just off the Boulder Turnpike). I have arranged for two conference rooms and a 16 mm projector for your use. We are planning to begin at 8:30 A.M. on January 21st.

We have made hotel reservations for you at the Holiday Inn Northglenn (303) 452-4100, located in Northglenn at I–25 and 120th Street. This facility is about 15 minutes due east of our location. Plan to take a taxi to the hotel, and I will see to it that you are provided with transportation from there.

Enclosed you will find informational literature about our company and, specifically, Employee Relations for your review. Please call me if you have questions about these details or matters relating to our workshop, Tony.

I look forward to meeting you on the 21st. Please forward your flight schedule, and I will contact you the evening of January 20th with any additional details.

Sincerely,

Elliott Payne
Training & Mgmt. Development
(303) 469-8844, WATS 525-8113

LETTERS ON IN-HOUSE AND OUTSIDE TRAINING PROGRAMS: SAMPLE FOUR

Mr. Steven O. Smythe
2100 West 100th Avenue
Denver, Colorado 80221

Dear Steve:

I am pleased to tell you that your manager has nominated you to be a participant in the in-company Technical Writing program to be held March 9–12, 19——.

Wilson Associates will present this practical workshop for persons who are data-oriented and who prepare specialized reports with technical content. Discussion, examples, and exercises will be tailored to meet the needs of workshop participants.

In this program, you will learn to define the purpose and scope of a report, collect, organize, and analyze data and adapt it to audience needs, and revise and edit reports to produce a good finished product. Dr. Terry Browne will conduct the workshop. More information is attached.

The program is 16 hours in length and will be conducted in half-day sessions from 1:00 to 5:00 P.M. each day in Conference Room "P." It is important that you attend all or none of these sessions, so please call me to confirm your participation. If this is not a convenient time, we can put you on the waiting list for the next program, to be held this summer.

Sincerely,

Margot Alexander
Training and Development Coordinator

LETTERS ON IN-HOUSE AND OUTSIDE
TRAINING PROGRAMS: SAMPLE FIVE

Mr. James D. Hanson
10 Longs Peak Drive
Broomfield, Colorado 80020

Dear Jim:

I am pleased to report that our pilot session of the "Managing Stress" program, conducted by Dr. Richard Hoerl during January, was a complete success.

As such, we have scheduled a second session with Dr. Hoerl for Thursday, March 18, from 8:15 A.M. to 12:15 P.M. in Conference Room "H."

Your name was on the waiting list for the program, and this letter is your confirmation of registration. If you are unable to attend for any reason, please call me to cancel so that we may fill your slot in the registration.

Dr. Hoerl suggests that you wear comfortable clothing for this session as he will be demonstrating some exercises.

We look forward to seeing you on the 18th.

Sincerely,

James Baker
Training and Development

LETTERS ON IN-HOUSE AND OUTSIDE
TRAINING PROGRAMS: SAMPLE SIX

TO: Distribution
FROM: Myron L. Treber
SUBJ: INTRODUCTION TO JCL CLASS

I am pleased to announce that as part of our Production Division training program, Walt Bayerle will be offering an Introduction to JCL class beginning on Monday, June 28th. Details are:

WHAT: Introduction to JCL

WHEN: Monday, June 28th, through Wednesday, June 30th from 4:00 P.M. to 12:00 midnight

WHERE: First Floor Classroom

The reason for the hours is to accommodate our Production shift employees.

Class size is limited to eight people, so enrollment will be on a first-come, first-served basis. Enroll by using our education enrollment form and turning it in to Marjie Young as soon as possible.

Thank you for your continued support of our training programs.

LETTERS ON IN-HOUSE AND OUTSIDE
TRAINING PROGRAMS: SAMPLE SEVEN

      TO: Distribution
FROM: Myron L. Treber
  SUBJ: MODEL-NETICS GRADUATION

This week marks the conclusion of our Model-Netics Training. According to my records, everyone completed at least 80 percent of the sessions with many of you having 100 percent attendance!

We are planning to "ceremonialize" at the Old Spaghetti Factory this Wednesday evening at 6:30 P.M. immediately following the last session.

Graduation ceremonies will take place after dinner with Curt Reed and Bill Harris presiding.

Please plan on joining us in order to receive your well-deserved diploma.

See you at the Old Spaghetti Factory on Wednesday at 6:30!

LETTERS ON IN-HOUSE AND OUTSIDE
TRAINING PROGRAMS: SAMPLE EIGHT

Mr. R. E. Hynes
General Manager
Ten Mile Lake
Post Office Box 302
Casper, Wyoming 82602

Dear Russ:

Attached, per your request, is a topical outline and schedule for the Mountain States Employers Council course, Supervisory Skills I, for the minerals and energy industry.

As you will recall from our discussion, we recommend the MSEC courses because our employee critiques have been excellent. In addition, the Council is a non-profit organization and we are members, which significantly impacts the cost. For example, the fee for the Supervisory Skills course is $90.00 per attendee, whereas the fee for the Industrial Personnel Management program is $330.00 per participant.

Also attached is a copy of the script for our new Career Programs presentation. Please review it and let us know if you would like to have this program, and the New Employee Orientation, presented at the Ten Mile Lake and Aspen Creek operations.

If you have any questions, please contact me.

Sincerely,

Mary F. Cook
Director
Employee Relations

LETTERS ON IN-HOUSE AND OUTSIDE
TRAINING PROGRAMS: SAMPLE NINE

> TO : All Managers
> FROM: Kenneth Wilson
> Vice-President Operations
> SUBJ: PERFORMANCE APPRAISAL WORKSHOP

Attached for your information is a program announcement on the Performance Appraisal Workshops to be held July 23, 27, and 28, at 9:00 A.M., in Conference Room "H."

Conducting performance appraisals in a timely and appropriate manner is a vital segment of our overall management philosophy. With that in mind, I encourage you to attend one of the workshops. Pick up your Performance Appraisal Forms and brush up on your appraisal skills.

Please direct any questions about the program to me.

LETTERS ON IN-HOUSE AND OUTSIDE
TRAINING PROGRAMS: SAMPLE TEN

> TO: All Managers
> FROM: Mary Cook
> Director, Employee Relations
> SUBJ: MANAGERS' ADMINISTRATIVE OVERVIEW PRESENTATION

During the past several weeks, we have been working on a presentation for new managers that reviews Company policies and procedures and is designed as an introduction to the management philosophy and style of our Company.

The first session will be held July 20th at 9:00 A.M. in our Auditorium. The overview will last approximately two and one-half hours. In addition, we have completed a New Employee Orientation form that will be shown at the same time. An agenda is attached for your information.

Please call Ruth Spanarella, ext. 2902, and let her know whether or not you plan to attend.

LETTERS ON IN-HOUSE AND OUTSIDE
TRAINING PROGRAMS: SAMPLE ELEVEN

> TO: All Employees
> FROM: Fred Foresberg
> Personnel Manager
> SUBJ: SEXUAL HARASSMENT WORKSHOP

As part of our Affirmative Action Program, we are conducting an in-house management development workshop for supervisors and managers on sexual harassment.

The workshop will define what sexual harassment is and a movie will be shown that depicts forms of sexual harassment that can occur on the job.

As a manager at Rankin Corporation, it is important for you to understand the problems experienced when sexual harassment occurs and to ensure that your department is free from any form of harassment.

This workshop will be held October 10th, from 9:00 A.M. to 4:00 P.M. in the auditorium. Please make plans to attend.

TO EMPLOYEE REGARDING DEADLINE
FOR APPLICATION TO
UNIVERSITY TECHNICAL PROGRAM

Mr. James C. Smythe
2301 Blake Street
Denver, Colorado 80202

     Re: Executive Program—Colorado School of Mines

Dear Jim:

The deadline for making application to the Mineral and Energy Executive Program II at the Colorado School of Mines is February 28.

The program is divided into two sessions: May 16 to 28 and July 26 to August 6, 19——.

Our nominee from last summer, John Lake, has evaluated the program very favorably. After receiving the promotional literature for this year, I talked with John to see if his perceptions were still true. He indicated that he still felt very good about the program, professors, and course content.

If you wish to nominate someone, or would like additional information, please let me know before mid-February.

Sincerely,

Elliot Payne
Training and Development

TO TRAINING COMPANY
DECLINING PURCHASE OF PROGRAM

Mr. Robert L. Browne
President
Dynamics Training Corporation
482 Congress Street
Portland, Maine 04101

Dear Mr. Browne:

Stewart Martin has forwarded your training material to us. We reviewed it and found it interesting. It looks like a very worthwhile program; however, it doesn't fit our needs at this time.

We will retain the information for future reference and appreciate your interest in Waltham Manufacturing Company. If you ever get to Denver, please drop by so we can discuss the future use of your programs—perhaps a 19—— timetable would be suitable.

Sincerely,

Mary F. Cook
Director
Employee Relations

TO UNIVERSITY REGARDING USE OF THEIR PROGRAM TO TRAIN EXECUTIVES

Mr. Robert L. Coe
Director, Management
Development Programs
The University of Utah
Salt Lake City, Utah 84112

Dear Mr. Coe:

We have received the information on your Executive Development Series, and we are impressed with the content and diversity of the program. I've talked with John Brown at The Wilson Company, and he speaks highly of your program.

We are in the process of looking at our new executives to determine who we will be developing for further promotion, and this process should be completed in September. We will begin our new development process in 19—— and will keep your program in mind.

I would appreciate your keeping me up to date on your schedules and the course content, as they change. Your interest in our Company is appreciated.

Sincerely,

Chet Wilson
Training and Development

REGARDING EXECUTIVE VIDEO TRAINING ON PRESENTATIONS

Mr. Donald R. Stegoe
The Television Workshop
39 West 55th Street
New York, New York 10019

Dear Don:

Our president, James T. Stevens, has asked that I get back to you now that he has had more time to consider your Executive Program.

Stan Johnson conducted a fine presentation. We were impressed with what you offer and might consider it in the future; however, at this time we have been invited to participate in a similar program in Los Angeles. This program will include ten of our executives, and the cost will be covered by one of our joint venture partners who conducts the workshops in-house on a regular basis.

Thanks again for the time you have taken in reviewing your services with us.

Sincerely,

Larry Smith
Executive Development

TO UNIVERSITY PROFESSOR CONFIRMING PARTICIPATION IN MANAGER OVERVIEW MEETING

Dr. Dale Meyer
College of Business Administration
University of Colorado
Boulder, Colorado 80302

Dear Dale:

We are very pleased that you have agreed to participate in our Managers' Meeting on March 23rd. It will be held at Stouffer's Denver Inn located in the airport complex.

We are bringing together all of our managers and supervisors to give them a fresh view of where we stand on various projects. The morning sessions will consist of three one-hour talks to be given by Congressman Tim Wirth; Dr. John Stoessinger, Presidential Professor at Colorado School of Mines; and Ms. Louise Dunlap, Executive Vice-President of the Environmental Policy Center in Washington, D.C.

Through the morning sessions, we hope to freshly sensitize the group to the realities of the world in which we function ... a sort of national, international, and local overview of politics and environmental concerns and their effect on the U.S. economy.

These morning sessions then set the stage for our small afternoon group sessions. The three afternoon programs will deal with our long-range plans, a review of our company's thrusts in the public sector, and the program you will be presenting on "The Management of Change." We feel that the success of all of our other efforts is dependent to a great degree on the ability of our people to work through conflict. We are looking forward to your participation in our meeting.

We'd be pleased to have you as our guest for lunch. A draft of our agenda is enclosed for your information.

Sincerely,

Mary F. Cook
Director
Employee Relations

TO FOUNDATION CONFIRMING REQUEST
TO SERVE ON A COMMITTEE

Mr. C. L. Barker, Chairman
Colorado Mining Association
  Education Foundation, Inc.
Denver Hilton Office Building
  Suite 410
1515 Cleveland Place
Denver, Colorado 80202

Dear Mr. Barker:

I would be pleased to serve on your Planning and Curriculum Committee for the Summer Field Course. Your application and promotional material on the program are excellent.

I look forward to becoming an active and contributing member of the Committee.

Please contact me on future Committee meeting dates.

Sincerely,

Robert L. Schaeffer
Manager
Employee Selection and Development

CONGRATULATIONS TO EMPLOYEE
ON COMPLETION OF MASTER'S THESIS

Mr. John Q. Birch
10207 West 101st Avenue
Pueblo, Colorado 80202

Dear John:

I've just learned that you have completed your master's thesis on "The Application of Borehole Gamma-Ray Logging in Non-Sandstone Uranium Deposits," and have been awarded your Master of Science Degree in Geology.

You are to be congratulated on your energy and perseverance at the conclusion of this extremely worthy goal, and for wrestling with a topic which I know was tough and bewildering and took a considerable period of time to complete.

Again, congratulations and good luck in your career!

Sincerely,

James L. Lindquist
President

CONFIRMATION OF SEMINAR REGISTRATION

Ms. Linda DeMera
10 Longs Peak Drive
Broomfield, Colorado 80020

Re: Confirmation—Seminar Registration

Dear Linda:

This is to confirm that you are registered for the Managing Management Time seminar, which will be held February 25 and 26, 19——, at Mountain States Employers Council, 1790 Logan Street, Denver.

You will need to make your own travel and hotel arrangements.

Please forward an approved Form 183 (Request for Disbursement) to my attention for processing. Cost is to be $160.00, and will be paid by the company.

We will appreciate your critique of the course upon its completion.

Sincerely,

Jane D. Jones
Training Coordinator

CONFIRMATION OF SEMINAR AND HOTEL DETAILS

TO: All Managers
FROM: Dan Thomas
SUBJ: SEMINAR AND HOTEL DETAILS

Enclosed are the prework, Effective Planning and Control and Understanding the Manager's Job for next week's program. Effective Planning and Control is a self-assessment exercise, and Understanding the Manager's Job is an analysis of your work objectives. Please complete both workbooks and bring them with you.

We encourage you to take plenty of time to complete the workbooks. Your personal "payoff" in the program will be enhanced if your prework reflects your style and your objectives. Since there will be some numerical analysis, please bring a pocket calculator with you to the seminar.

HOTEL ARRANGEMENTS

The hotel is the Holiday Inn—Northglenn, located at I-25 and 120th Ave. We have single rooms confirmed in your names for Tuesday evening. Plan to check into your rooms after the first day's session. Hotel and meals are to be covered on your individual expense account.

The hotel has excellent recreational facilities, including indoor pool, saunas, and Jacuzzi. As a guest, you have access to Northglenn's recreation building adjacent to the hotel, which includes indoor track, racquetball, and basketball. There is also an outdoor jogging track behind the hotel. The hotel telephone number is 452-4100.

Dress is casual. The program will begin at 8:20 A.M. on Tuesday, February 2nd, and will adjourn by 4:00 P.M. Thursday, February 4th.

Give me a call if you have any questions about the program.

TO UNIVERSITY PROFESSOR REGARDING PERFORMANCE OF COOPERATIVE EDUCATION STUDENT

Mr. John Phillips
Summer Placement Director
Colorado School of Mines
Golden, Colorado 80401

Dear John:

Since Kevin Wilson started working with us early this year, he has been involved in the selection of equipment for the Rolling Hills project. Kevin's primary function has been to calculate annual volumes of overburden, parting, rehandle material, and coal, using equipment specifications and geologic data. This task has involved the production of various computer and hand-generated cross-sections, isopachs, and range diagrams. He has also tabulated the annual cost data from given unit costs and production rates for various equipment fleets.

Kevin has received instruction on various computer applications that he has used to generate computer products. He has met with manufacturers' representatives and applications engineers to gain their input on his proposals. He has visited the Rolling Hills mine, helped our engineers with calculations for various projects, and directed part of the drafting work for the equipment selection reports.

Kevin's time has been budgeted into many of our planned future projects as a very necessary and important part, and he will be used to the extent that he is capable to help successfully complete the projects. Some of the things he will be doing in the future are overall project mine planning, completing work at operating mines, financial analyses of mining ventures, and report writing.

Kevin is a superior performer, and we are pleased to have him working in our summer program.

Sincerely,

Elaine Sutter
Summer Program Manager

EVALUATION OF TRAINING PROGRAMS:
SAMPLE ONE

Mr. Harold M. Schlut
Box 10A
Casper, Wyoming 82604

Dear Harold:

Please take some time to complete the attached evaluation of our March Performance Appraisal Workshop. I am interested in your perceptions of the program and whether you feel you have been able to apply any of the information back on the job. Your input will be helpful in planning future programs.

Two days is barely enough time to introduce you to some ideas about supervision and give you some feedback about your personal style. What happens after the program is really up to you and your supervisor. With this in mind, we briefed the department heads on Friday of that week on what we had covered in the Workshop, and then gave them feedback on issues that you as a group had raised.

For me, all five days were most productive. Let me know through the evaluation if you agree and what you think could be done to improve future programs.

Sincerely,

Susan Granger
Training Director

EVALUATION OF TRAINING PROGRAMS:
SAMPLE TWO

Skilldex, Inc.
5310 Harvest Hill Road
  Suite 120
Post Office Box 113
Dallas, Texas 75230

Gentlemen:

Carolyn Gregg, one of our Land Secretaries, attended your "Basic Skills for the Land Secretary" program in Denver on September 9th.

Her written evaluation and follow-up debriefing of the seminar were highly complimentary and most positive. I must admit to a personal bias against one-day, "catch-all" programs, but yours is evidently a major exception. Congratulations on such a fine, results-oriented seminar.

Please extend my thanks to all three presenters, and send me dates for future Denver programs.

Sincerely,

E. E. Payne
Training and Development

DETAILED REPORT OF TRAINING ACTIVITIES
PROVIDED TO VICE-PRESIDENT
OF HUMAN RESOURCES

Mr. Thomas V. Mann
Vice-President
Human Resources
Horn Manufacturing Company
One River Front Drive
Chicago, Illinois 60611

Dear Tom:

Attached for your information are the current Training and Management Development Activity Reports for the fourth quarter and for year-end.

The month of December typically is a light month for training and development. There was a Performance Appraisal Workshop in-house, and 18 persons attended seminars and professional meetings outside the company.

The year-end summary illustrates the diversity of training and management development activities. Approximately 100 employees participated in our Tuition Refund Program, with 12 of them actively pursuing graduate degrees. A list of those persons, and their areas of study, is included in the attachments.

In-company programs expanded during the year to 13, with over 700 employee registrations in these programs. The total direct cost was under $40,000.

Additional highlights for the year included:

- Over 75 managers/supervisors attended one of five Performance Appraisal Workshops.
- Eight new in-company programs were developed.
- Thirty-five supervisors from California attended in-company Labor Relations Workshops.
- Careers Advisory Committee sponsored Careers Week and College Day, attended by 17 area colleges.

Much time was spent during 19—— investigating and planning management development and general employee development programs for implementation.

Sincerely,

Jeanne Morgan
Personnel Manager

5

Letters That Foster Good Employee Relations

Good employee relations are maintained when employee communications are honest, straightforward, understandable, timely, and caring.

When you write a letter to employees, set it aside for an hour or so, go back, pick it up, and read it as though you were an employee who has received the letter. How do you feel about it?

MANAGERS' TIPS FOR POSITIVE EMPLOYEE RELATIONS LETTERS

- For positive employee relations, write your letters in the same way you would talk to employees face to face. Don't "talk down" to them; on the other hand, don't use a lot of big words and pompous sentences.

- Many organizations still use a very formal style when inviting employees to parties and other social functions. Such formality is passé. A casual, warm style is more in keeping with the values of today's workers.

- When explaining a company policy, a layoff, or facility shutdown, remember that there are three objectives to this type of communication:
  1. To inform.
  2. To set out all details, including benefits and restrictions.
  3. To be considerate of employees' feelings while communicating your message.

TO ADVISORY COMMITTEE REGARDING
LUNCH HOSTED BY THE PRESIDENT

TO: Training and Development Advisory Committee
FROM: Mary M. White
SUBJ: LUNCHEON DETAILS

We'd be pleased if you could join us for lunch on Friday, January 4, at the Rolling Hills Country Club. The luncheon will be hosted by our president, Bob Johnson, and senior vice-president, Leonard Smith.

There is a twofold purpose: The first is to thank all of you for the assistance and support you provided the Training and Development function. The second is to receive feedback from each of you concerning accomplishments this past year and suggestions for next year's training and development activities.

Please confirm your attendance by December 23.

TO DEPARTMENT HEADS
REGARDING NEW FLEXIBLE WORK WEEK

TO: All Department Heads, Managers and Supervisors

Security Life has successfully operated on a four-day week basis for the last several years. We will now expand the options as we operate on a flexible work week basis. The flexible work week offers a wide variety of work schedules within the basic work week, including a four-day work week.

The office is open from 7:00 A.M. to 5:00 P.M., Monday through Friday. Supervisors are to work with their people in setting the work week, taking into consideration the following:

1. Schedules are within the 7:00–5:00 time frame; core hours (when everyone is to be in the office) are 9:06 A.M. - 2:54 P.M.
2. Each person must work 37 hours a week.
3. Not less than ½ hour or more than one hour should be taken for lunch.
4. Once the hours are established, the schedule is semi-permanent. The person is to work the same schedule each week, unless or until the person and his/her supervisor agree to a change.

Sincerely,

Barbara L. Allen
Asst. Vice-President, Personnel

TO ALL EMPLOYEES REGARDING SUMMER
WORK SCHEDULE: SAMPLE ONE

TO: All Denver Area Employees
FROM: John C. Wilson
SUBJ: SUMMER WORK SCHEDULE

In order to provide employees with extended weekend hours during the summer months, effective Monday, June 8, and continuing through Friday, September 4, we will work the normal hours of 8:00 A.M. to 5:00 P.M.; however, we will shorten the lunch period to one half-hour daily and will leave work at 2:30 P.M. on Fridays. As a result of this change, employees will work 8½ hours Monday through Thursday and 6 hours Friday. For employees affected by this change, overtime will be paid for all hours in excess of 40 in a week.

If this change should cause a problem for you, please discuss the problem with your supervisor so that a mutually agreeable solution may be worked out.

We've looked at several alternative work schedules, including a 7:30 A.M. to 4:30 P.M. work day. However, the time differences with other organizations with whom we do business have made the 8:00 to 5:00 schedule the most feasible for our efficient operation.

Employees are encouraged to continue to participate in our fitness programs. The schedules for the Fitness Center and Health Unit activities will be adjusted to accommodate the new work schedule and will be posted. As before, you are reminded that the time spent using the Fitness Center during working hours must be made up during the same week. It is expected that prior arrangements be made with your supervisor to cover the workload.

The noontime programs will move to Wednesday during the summer. A new schedule will be published.

To prevent a possible overload in the cafeteria, department managers may wish to stagger lunch times in their areas. The cafeteria is open from 11:30 A.M. to 1:00 P.M., except for the deli, which will remain open until 1:30 P.M.

In order for the program to be successful, it is important that the 30-minute lunch period and the new hours be closely observed. Your cooperation in this regard is necessary to ensure the continuation of this summer program.

TO ALL EMPLOYEES REGARDING SUMMER
WORK SCHEDULE: SAMPLE TWO

TO: All Employees
FROM: Holly Johnson
SUBJ: SUMMER WORK SCHEDULES

Last year, there were several problems associated with the summer hours schedule, and that schedule will not be repeated this year.

Currently there are two schedules being considered for this summer:

1. A 7:30 A.M. to 4:00 P.M. workday with one half-hour for lunch, or
2. Maintain our regular hours of 8:00 A.M. to 5:00 P.M., with a one-hour lunch period.

The shortened lunch period would not affect those individuals who periodically must conduct business during the lunch hour. If the 7:30 to 4:00 schedule is chosen and it creates undue hardship (such as babysitting problems), an alternative schedule can be worked out with your manager.

Please indicate your choice of a summer schedule and return the completed form to Personnel by March 24, 19——.

....

RETURN TO THE PERSONNEL DEPT. BY MARCH 24, 19——.

The summer hours schedule I prefer is checked below:

——   7:30 A.M.–4:00 P.M. with one half-hour lunch
——   8:00 A.M.–5:00 P.M. with one-hour lunch

Comments: _____

_____

_____

_____

TO MANAGERS REGARDING SUMMER SCHEDULE SURVEY

      TO: L. G. Dunn
    FROM: Holly Johnson
           Personnel Manager
    SUBJ: SUMMER SCHEDULE SURVEY

Here are the results of the RME employee schedule survey:

7:30 A.M. to 4:00 P.M. w/one half-hour lunch	211
8:00 A.M. to 4:30 P.M. w/one half-hour lunch	30
8:00 A.M. to 5:00 P.M. w/one-hour lunch	24
	265

This represents a 70 percent response. Ballots with comments are available in my office.

With your permission, we will announce the 7:30 A.M. to 4:00 P.M. work schedule for the summer.

ANNOUNCING A PROMOTION

TO: All Employees
FROM: J. R. Brooks
SUBJ: PROMOTION

I am pleased to announce the promotion of John A. Lange to the position of manager, Market Research, effective immediately. In his new role, John will have responsibility for our economic and marketing analysis activities in all minerals and will continue to report directly to me.

John joined Rankin in 19—— as a mineral economist. He continued in Market Research until February 1981 when he was promoted to marketing coordinator in the Coal Diversification group. John's most recent assignment was manager, Market Research—Coal.

Bill Bradley has moved into the position of staff market analyst. As such, he will maintain his current lead role in the coal and other minerals areas. Bill will report to John along with David McLean, Susan Mahoney, and Tom Hendrickson.

ANNOUNCING A CAREER DAY

TO: All Casper, Wyoming Employees
FROM: D. C. Lewis
SUBJ: CAREER DAY

Career Day for Casper Exploration and General Services employees has been scheduled for Friday, December 14th.

The program will last approximately 45 minutes and will consist of the Career Programs slide presentation, distribution of a Career Planning Workbook, and a question-and-answer period.

There will be two sessions: one held at the Casper Exploration office at 1:30 P.M. and the other in the General Services office at 2:45 P.M.

We're looking forward to seeing you!

SENDING NEW INFORMATION AND THANKING PREVIOUS CHAIRPERSON

Ms. Jackie L. Ullmer
93 Paul Revere Road
Needham, Massachusetts 02194

Dear Jackie:

Since you were the very able and active chairperson for our Career Programs Advisory Committee last year, I thought you would be interested in seeing the CAREER PROGRAMS poster and flyer we had designed this year. The Advisory

Committee worked on the project, and we had a Career Day that turned out quite well … more than 200 people attended and more than 75 people entered the poster-coloring contest. I've enclosed a poster for you.

We miss you and look forward to your return. We hope you are enjoying the current semester at MIT.

Best wishes for a happy holiday season!

Sincerely,

Mary F. Cook
Director, Employee Relations

ANSWERING EMPLOYEE SERVICE AWARDS QUERY

Ms. Mary Wonder
Supervisor, Community Relations
Canadian Coal, Ltd.
Post Office Box 2000
Sparwood, British Columbia
Canada VOB 2G0

Dear Ms. Wonder:

Your recent letter to Mr. Nelson inquiring about our methods of rewarding employees for their years of service has been forwarded to me for reply.

Our company holds a dinner-dance each year shortly before Christmas. At this time, our president presents awards to those employees who have passed five-year milestones with the company.

Five years:	Cross 14K gold pen and pencil set engraved with employee's name.
Ten years:	AM/FM digital clock/radio, with plate attached, engraved with employee's name and hire date.
Fifteen years:	Gold Seiko or Bulova watch, engraved with employee's name and hire date.
Twenty years:	Portable television set, with plate attached, engraved with employee's name, hire date, and "20-Year Service Award."
Twenty-five years:	Videotape recorder.

I hope this information is what you need. Please let me know if you have any questions.

Sincerely,

Holly Wolmsley
Employee Benefits Coordinator

CONGRATULATIONS ON ANNIVERSARY
WITH COMPANY

Ms. Lynn Cottle
3427 South Elm Court
Chicago, Illinois 60657

Dear Lynn:

Congratulations on your fifth anniversary with Rankin Corporation.

We appreciate your many good efforts on behalf of the company and hope that we celebrate many more anniversaries together.

Sincerely,

John P. Rankin
President

FORWARDING PAYMENT
FOR MUSIC AT COMPANY PARTY

Mr. Tommy Hancock
Super Natural Family Band
2040 South Lincoln Street
Beaumont, Texas 77702

Dear Tommy:

Attached is our check in the amount of $350.00, covering the balance of the amount due for your services at our dinner-dance at the Regency Hotel on December 13th.

We want you to know that your music contributed much toward a delightful evening. Comments received from our people the next day were very enthusiastic— so much so that as soon as we can set a date for our service awards dinner-dance in December of 19——, we will be contacting you about playing for us again.

Sincerely,

Lloyd R. Cooke
Director
Human Resources

ANNOUNCEMENT OF COMPANY PICNIC

TO: All Employees
FROM: John Enrick
       Personnel Manager
SUBJ: COMPANY PICNIC

There will be a company picnic at McLaren Park on August 17, from 10:00 A.M. until 3:00 P.M. The company will furnish beer, pop, hamburgers, hot dogs, buns, and chips. Each family should bring a covered dish, either salad or vegetable. Tables will be set up buffet-style for food service.

Softball, volleyball, and croquet equipment will be available.

Please join us for a day of fun in the park, and be sure to bring the kids! We'll have sack races, an egg toss, etc., and prizes will be awarded to children who participate in the games.

Call Jean Collins on extension 320 for picnic reservations.

CONFIRMING COMPANY PARTICIPATION IN SUPPORT OF EMPLOYEE BOWLING LEAGUE

Mr. Bill Shumane
Brown Engineering Company
Box 200
Orlando, Florida 32802

Dear Bill:

I'm following up on your memo and our telephone conversation with regard to the Orlando Bowling League. I have reviewed your request with management and am pleased to confirm the following support for your league:

The company will pay the cost of shirts, with logos, and any sponsor's fees.

It will be up to each employee to pay bowling costs and association fees.

It is our understanding that you will have both a men's and a women's league, and that the leagues are open to all employees.

Please send a Request for Disbursement form to me for approval when you're ready. If you have any questions, don't hesitate to give me a call.

Best wishes for a winning season!

Sincerely,

David Gifford
Employee Relations

CONDOLENCES ON DEATH OF EMPLOYEE'S SPOUSE

Mr. John K. Kennedy
1632 Sunset Boulevard
Los Angeles, California 91607

Dear John:

Please accept our sincere condolences on the death of your wife. Words cannot express the sorrow we feel. We want you to know that our thoughts and prayers are with you.

If there is anything we can do to help you during this time of sorrow, please call on us.

Sincerely,

Harold M. Morrow
Personnel Manager
The Samson Company

CONGRATULATIONS ON PROMOTION

TO:	Robert M. Browne
	Manager, Information Systems
FROM:	Harold M. Morrow
	Personnel Director
SUBJ:	PROMOTION

Bob, congratulations on your recent promotion to manager of the Information Systems Department.

Your diligence and hard work have paid off, and we are pleased that you have accepted this new job with such enthusiasm.

If I can be of any assistance to you in your new position, please let me know.

LETTER OF RECOMMENDATION
OF FORMER EMPLOYEE

To Whom It May Concern:

Ms. Martha K. Stephens worked for The Brown Engineering Company from September 19—— to January 19—— as manager of our General Records Department. During this time, I had occasion to work closely with her on various projects involving the design and implementation of record-keeping procedures.

Martha proved herself to have extremely well developed and highly efficient problem-solving skills. She is well organized and operates within the superior level in the administrative area. She approaches tasks in an extremely systematic and analytical fashion and has excellent skills in collecting data and integrating it into a workable plan.

Martha has a unique ability to perform research and report the results of that research in a usable format. She is a competent individual with very good interpersonal skills, allowing her to work well at all corporate levels and displaying flexibility in her approach to people.

She has an outstanding knowledge of the records-management activity, works well under pressure, is reliable, and is a good manager of people. I highly recommend her for any position for which she applies and for which she qualifies.

Sincerely,

Vincent Gorman
Personnel Manager

6

Letters That Promote
Good Community Relations

Most companies understand the need to promote good community relations. Individuals and other organizations located in the same area as your facilities should know your organizational style. Are you a good corporate citizen? How do you treat your employees? How do you handle environmental problems? Are you a socially responsible organization?

A pro-active community relations program will go a long way toward projecting a positive organizational image.

MANAGER'S TIPS ON COMMUNITY RELATIONS
COMMUNICATIONS

- A pro-active approach to a new community—one where you intend to open a new facility—might include letters introducing your company to:
  —the mayor, city council, and county commissioners,
  —fire and police officials in your area,
  —hospitals and doctors within the immediate vicinity,
  —local newspapers and TV news media, and
  —local charitable organizations with whom you may participate in fund drives; the United Way would be an example.

- It's important to tell your own employees as much as you tell outside organizations and individuals.

TO MAYOR OF TOWN ANNOUNCING
NEW FACILITY TO BE CONSTRUCTED

The Honorable John L. Meyer
Mayor of Buffalo
Buffalo, Wyoming 82834

Dear Sir:

We plan to open a coal mine outside Buffalo that will employ 650 people. We hired an independent consulting firm to complete a socio-economic impact study of the area, which I am enclosing for your information.

As you will see, the study details the need for new housing, schools, and sewers, and our company would like to meet with you and the Town Council to work out mutually agreeable details of what will be a significant growth opportunity for the town of Buffalo. It is our intent to work closely with you and the people of Buffalo to minimize any dislocation that might result from our new mining operation.

I will call you next week for an appointment. In the meantime, if you have questions on the study, please give me a call at the above number.

Sincerely,

Owen Paschal
Director of Operations

TO CHAIRPERSON OF CITY COUNCIL
ANNOUNCING NEW FACILITY
AND REQUESTING IMPROVEMENTS

Ms. Kathy M. Donahue
Chairperson
The Denver City Council
City and County Building
Denver, Colorado 80202

Dear Ms. Donahue:

The Langworth Corporation is planning to open a new manufacturing facility in Montbello Park at 4800 Colorado Boulevard. We would like to enlist the support of the Denver City Council in continuing development of the Montbello area adjacent to our property.

We plan to improve the area that borders Smith Road, and we would be happy to share the costs of paving that road to the end of 48th Street on the north side.

We are pleased to be a new industry in the community and hope to contribute to the local economy by providing jobs and revenues.

I would like to meet with you or your representative at a mutually convenient time regarding these improvements.

Sincerely,

Joseph R. Walston
President
Langworth Corporation

TO LOCAL DOCTOR ADVISING
OF NEW PLANT AND NEED FOR
PRE-EMPLOYMENT PHYSICAL EXAMINATIONS

Dr. John W. Downing
3700 Center Street
Eugene, Oregon 97405

Dear Dr. Downing:

We plan to open a new manufacturing plant in Eugene that will employ approximately 400 people. We require a pre-employment physical examination and would like you to conduct these examinations for us, if you can handle the numbers of people we expect to hire.

Our initial employment will be 100 persons. We then plan to hire 50 people per week until we reach our full complement of 800 employees.

I would like to meet with you as soon as possible to discuss the contents of the physical examination and the cost per person. I would appreciate your calling me when you can get together.

We need to finalize all arrangements by August 24th.

Sincerely,

Bradley T. Tower
Personnel Manager

TO SCHOOL DISTRICT ON
PARTNERSHIP TRAINING AGREEMENT

Ms. Asahi Oshima
Boulder Valley School District
6500 East Arapahoe
Boulder, Colorado 80303

Dear Ms. Oshima:

The partnership between Browne Oil Company and Broomfield High School is making excellent strides. At your request, I am providing a summary of the activities scheduled for the 19——–19—— year.

December 13, 19——

The Broomfield High School Show Choir presented a Christmas musical for Browne Oil Company employees.

January 5, 19——

A "World-of-Work" training session was conducted for the students of the Wage-Earning Home Economics class. The session was taught by members of our Employee Relations Department.

Second Semester, 19——

A shadow program is currently being developed that will provide several students an opportunity to observe the day-to-day activities of selected professional employees. I will send you a progress report after the program is implemented.

Our involvement with the partnership is very rewarding, and we appreciate being participants in the program.

If you have additional questions, please call me.

Sincerely,

Myrna D. Mourning
Administrative-Manpower Planning
   and Affirmative Action Programs

TO BANK PRESIDENT COMMENTING ON SERVICE

Mr. Brad Stelling
Executive Vice-President
United Bank of Broomfield
No. 2 Garden Center
Broomfield, Colorado 80020

Dear Brad:

I just wanted to take this opportunity to let you know that, without exception, I have had the finest banking service I have experienced in many years as a result of my recent dealings with the United Bank of Broomfield.

The service has been outstanding. I can leave our building, go to the bank, make a deposit, and be back in the office within 10 to 15 minutes. We have had similar reports from all around the company, and I thought since you probably hear all of the complaints and few of the accolades, you might be happy to have my comments.

Sincerely,

Mary F. Cook
Director, Human Resources

TO FIRE CHIEF ADVISING OF NEW PLANT

Chief Don Snow
Durango Fire Department
Durango, Colorado 81301

Dear Chief Snow:

Our Company is planning to build a new manufacturing facility in Durango in the summer of 19——. Because of the size of the facility and the number of people we will house there, I am sure you will have concerns that it be built with the highest safety standards and concerns in mind.

We would like you to see our plans and meet our plant manager, Lynn Williams, and our Safety/Security manager, John Turco, as we make plans to start construction of the facility.

We plan to be in Durango on December 9th and would be able to meet with you on that date if that is possible. We will call the week before to confirm a time for the meeting.

We look forward to building our new facility in Durango and to making a positive contribution to the economic base and to the community at large.

We look forward to meeting you.

Sincerely,

Landon Miles
Vice-President, Operations
Rocky Mountain Manufacturing, Inc.

TO POLICE CHIEF ADVISING OF NEW PLANT

Chief Ralph Fenton
Durango Police Department
Durango, Colorado 81301

Dear Chief Fenton:

Our Company is planning to build a new manufacturing facility in Durango in the summer of 19——. Because we will be manufacturing a valuable product that is easily resold if stolen, and because some of the materials that go into making the product are precious metals, we are naturally very concerned for the security of the facility.

We would like you to see our plans for security for the plant and to meet our plant manager, Lynn Williams, and our Safety/Security manager, John Turco, as we make plans to start construction of the facility.

We plan to be in Durango on December 9th and would be able to meet with you on that date. We also plan to meet with Chief Don Snow on the same date. Perhaps the two of you could coordinate the times. We will call you both the week before to confirm the meetings.

We look forward to building our new facility in Durango and to making a positive contribution to the economic base and to the community at large, and look forward to meeting you.

Sincerely,

Landon Miles
Vice-President, Operations
Rocky Mountain Manufacturing, Inc.

TO EDITOR OF PAPER ANNOUNCING NEW PLANT

Mr. Robert M. Moore
Editor
<u>Durango Times</u>
Durango, Colorado 81301

Dear Mr. Moore:

Our Company is planning to build a new manufacturing facility in Durango in the summer of 19——. We will employ approximately 350 people at full capacity, and will commence hiring approximately January 10, 19——.

We would like you to be aware of our plans and will keep you up to date as we progress from the construction through the hiring phases.

We will be in Durango on December 9th to meet with members of the community, the mayor, and the fire and police chiefs, and would be happy to spend some time with you to share our plans. We will call you the week before to confirm a time for a meeting.

We look forward to building our new facility in Durango and to making a positive contribution to your economic base and to the community at large, and will appreciate any publicity on our new venture that you can give us.

Sincerely,

Landon Miles
Vice-President, Operations
Rocky Mountain Manufacturing, Inc.

MEMORANDUM REGARDING VISITORS AND PLANT TOUR ARRANGEMENTS

TO: Robert Anselco
    VP, Operations

FROM: Lynn Lucero
      Director, Human Resources

SUBJ: COMMUNITY RELATIONS, VISITORS, AND TOURS

As a partner in the communities where the Company operates, it is important that our plants be receptive to visits by individuals or groups from educational institutions, civic organizations, and professional societies. The scheduling of tours or visits, however, should be coordinated to avoid unnecessary disruptions to production and to provide the best image of the Company from an operating standpoint.

Individual tours of operations can best be arranged by the manager responsible for that operation. Group tours should be coordinated by an assigned individual, after approval by the appropriate personnel manager and plant manager.

The coordinator will be responsible for securing guides to escort the tour groups and to make any other necessary arrangements for the tour. Guides are normally selected from among the managers familiar with the operations or areas to be visited.

Because of safety precautions, tours will be limited to adults and young adults (generally, age 15 and over). Where teen-age groups are accepted, the requesting group will be asked to supply adequate adult sponsors based on the ages of those in the group.

Tours by customer groups, field sales representatives, or dealer salespeople will be handled by the vice-president of sales.

If there are questions regarding plant tours, please direct them to our department.

**TO VICE-PRESIDENT REGARDING
EMPLOYEES' COMMUNITY INVOLVEMENT**

TO: Robert Anselco
        VP, Operations
FROM: Lynn Lucero
        Director, Human Resources
SUBJ: EMPLOYEES' COMMUNITY INVOLVEMENT

Each business or industry becomes a partner in the communities where its facilities are located. As a good partner in the communities where we do business, it is our company policy to involve members of the staff in community activities where their business judgment can be used to good advantage.

We believe that involvement is beneficial to the individual in a long-range, self-development program. We also believe there is value to the company in the contribution made by participants to keep these civic groups serving the basic social and economic needs for which they are intended.

Included in this area would be leadership activities or committee assignments in groups such as the following:

1. Industrial associations
2. Chambers of Commerce
3. Annual or capital fund drives (United Way, Red Cross, colleges, hospitals, health associations, etc.)
4. School districts and college or university advisory committees
5. Scholarship committees
6. Boy Scouts, Girl Scouts, YMCA, YWCA, and other youth associations
7. Professional groups (purchasing agents, traffic people, personnel, industrial engineers, etc.)
8. Jaycee and Jr. Achievement groups
9. Housing committees
10. Political advisory committees
11. Conference or convention committees
12. Human relations councils

Representation in any activity where time off from work is required should be coordinated with the employee's immediate supervisor.

The Director of Personnel and Industrial Relations will be responsible for encouraging members of management to participate in community activities, and will maintain appropriate records of our involvement. The plant personnel manager will be responsible for administering this policy at our various plants.

LETTER REGARDING COMPANY VOLUNTEER ACTIVITIES

Ms. Dee Relyea
Coordinator
Colorado Alliance of Business
24 Grant Street
Denver, Colorado 80203

Dear Dee:

I have thoroughly enjoyed my volunteer activities as an instructor for the "World of Work" orientations at the local high schools.

This is a very worthwhile project, and I look forward to the fall sessions with enthusiasm. I am committed to helping young people prepare themselves for the workplace.

Sincerely,

Myrna D. Mourning
EEO Coordinator

TO EMPLOYEES REGARDING U. S. SAVINGS BOND DRIVE

TO: All Employees
FROM: William L. Blaine
SUBJ: U.S. SAVINGS BONDS

We are pleased to announce that commencing July 1st the company is adding a new benefit for employees by offering payroll deduction for U.S. Savings Bonds.

In past years the interest rates paid on U.S. Savings Bonds were so low that we did not feel they were a viable savings vehicle to offer employees. That is not the case today. We feel that U.S. Savings Bonds are an excellent investment and are proud to include the payroll deduction feature as one of our many excellent employee benefits.

A Savings Bond pamphlet is enclosed for your information. You may contact Dianne Lewis in the Employee Relations Department for further information. If you would like to take advantage of the payroll deduction option that is available, you may obtain an authorization card from Dianne.

**THANK YOU TO EMPLOYEE WHO WILL
REPRESENT THE COMPANY IN BOND DRIVE**

Mr. Harold Babcock
President
Denver Equipment Company
107 Santa Fe Drive
Denver, Colorado 80404

Dear Mr. Babcock:

You are invited to attend the 19—— U.S. Savings Bonds Campaign Kickoff
Breakfast at the Denver Country Club. Your presence at the breakfast, January 27,
19——, from 7:45 A.M. to 9:15 A.M., will help us launch this worthy Campaign. Our
guest speaker will be Steven R. Mead, executive director of the U.S. Savings Bonds
Division, Washington, D.C.

This year, we are anticipating a favorable response to the Savings Bonds Campaign
effort as a result of the significant changes making the U.S. Savings Bonds a
variable rate instrument.

I hope you or your representative will be able to join us. Please return the enclosed
RSVP form by January 12, 19——.

Sincerely,

David S. Bizenski

**TO EMPLOYEES REGARDING
UNITED WAY DRIVE: SAMPLE ONE**

Dear Employees:

Your outstanding support of the United Way in past years has demonstrated your
commitment to helping others to Barnett Company management and to your
community. As we approach our annual United Way campaign, I ask that we
reaffirm together our commitment and community spirit.

This year, we have been selected to join with several other area businesses to "set
the pace" for the community. While the annual United Way campaign begins in the
fall, as a "Pacesetter Company" our campaign begins in July. A "Pacesetter
Company" is one that commits to an increase of at least 20 percent over last year's
contribution.

Contributions to United Way enable 85 human care agencies to provide valuable
services in the five-county metropolitan area. Hot meals for senior citizens, homes
for battered or abused children, visiting nurses for the disabled, and care and

education for the mentally and physically handicapped are but a few of the 200 different types of helping services offered by United Way agencies.

Please join me in supporting this worthwhile community effort.

Sincerely,

Edgard Rutherford
President

TO EMPLOYEES REGARDING UNITED WAY DRIVE: SAMPLE TWO

Dear Employee:

Your outstanding support of United Way last year was most gratifying in demonstrating to the community our employees' serious commitment to this most worthy cause. I would like to encourage you to continue with that enthusiasm as we begin our 19—— campaign.

Last year, our employees increased their contributions by 27 percent. Clearly, that was exemplary, and we hope for another significant increase this year. I feel confident that together we can achieve this worthy goal.

The total United Way goal for 19—— is $20,450,000 to support 76 agencies in 270 locations. You might think of your dollars as insignificant in light of that goal, but they are not. They provide hot meals for senior citizens who badly need them, homes for battered or abused children, and help for the physically disabled in our community.

Our campaign will be conducted during October. You will shortly be given a pledge card. I encourage you to participate by returning the card with your pledge to your department head or United Way representative.

Please give this your serious consideration. Working together, we can make United Way work for everyone.

Sincerely,

Lyndon B. Worth
President

TO EMPLOYEES REGARDIING UNITED WAY DRIVE: SAMPLE THREE

TO:	All Employees
FROM:	Kathy Langston
SUBJ:	19—— UNITED WAY CAMPAIGN

Recently Mr. Jefferson wrote to you about our 19—— United Way campaign goal of $25,000 in employee pledges. To kick off the campaign, we are holding a series of meetings on Thursday and Friday, October 1 and 2. So that we can avoid having entire departments at one meeting at one time, we have simply divided the company into four groups alphabetically. Please try to attend at the time indicated for the first letter of your last name. Of course, if you can't attend at that time, you are welcome to attend another session.

A–D   9:00 A.M., Thursday, October 1
E–K   10:00 A.M., Thursday, October 1
L–R   9:00 A.M., Friday, October 2
S–Z   10:00 A.M., Friday, October 2

All sessions will be held in Conference Room "A."

The meeting will consist of introductory remarks, a presentation by Norm Compton (a loaned executive from Conoco), details of the campaign, and a film about the work of the United Way.

Last year, our employees contributed $17,000, and the Company $5,000 to the United Way. Attached is a breakdown of how that $17,000 may have been utilized by United Way agencies. It is a graphic illustration of how much good our dollars really can do when united with the dollars of others.

With a fair share contribution from everyone, we will surpass our $25,000 goal easily. Scoreboards will be placed at various locations in the building so that we can see how we stand.

Help us help others—so that when the campaign is over, we can say to each of you, "Thanks to YOU, it really works for all of US."

THANKING EMPLOYEE FOR RUNNING
THE UNITED WAY CAMPAIGN FOR THE COMPANY

Mr. Robert M. Lein
10840 32nd Avenue
Golden, Colorado 80401

Dear Bob:

I certainly appreciate the enthusiastic spirit in which you are taking over our 19—— United Way Campaign.

Judy Weber and Ruth Browne will give you any assistance they can, as I will be gone the week that you have your meetings.

After the campaign is wrapped up, I would appreciate your forwarding for our files the United Way packet and a summary of how you ran the campaign this year so that we will be able to pass the information on to next year's Mile High executive.

Thanks again for your good efforts.

Sincerely,

Larry T. Thomas
Director of Personnel

TO CORPORATE OFFICER ADVISING OF INCREASE IN CONTRIBUTIONS TO UNITED WAY

Mr. L. O. Halleron
Treadwell Industries
400 Park Avenue
New York, New York 10022

Dear Len:

We are in the process of winding up our United Fund drive for 19—— and are pleased to report a significant increase in our contribution this year.

We are in the process of winding up our United Way drive for 19—— and are pleased to report a significant increase in our contribution this year.

	Gift	Per Capita	% Participation
19——	$25,293	$43.77	40%
19——	$18,651	$14.73	10%
19——	$10,316	$28.77	43%

The number of employees participating increased from 38 percent to 41 percent, and the amount of the gifts and the overall contribution also increased.

Mr. Robert M. Lein, manager of Planning and Analysis, was our United Way Chairman this year, and we are grateful to him for the fine effort he put forth.

Sincerely,

Larry T. Thomas
Director of Personnel

REQUEST FOR FUNDS FOR CHARITABLE GROUP

Mr. Reid Watson
Chairman, Contributions Committee
Hamilton Oil Company
Houston, Texas 77020

Dear Reid:

I understand that I have been given the responsibility for Corporate Contributions, and I would like officially to request that you consider the Volunteers of America as you consider contributions for the coming year.

As you know, I am on the Advisory Board of the VOA. It is my feelng that the VOA provides the very best of community programs and is one of the best-run charitable organizations in Houston. The Meals on Wheels program for senior citizens, for example, feeds over 16,000 senior citizens in the Houston area their one hot meal each day. This program is in need of financial support. I would like to suggest a $5,000 contribution for 19——.

If you would like me to attend a Board meeting and explain further details of the VOA programs, I would be happy to do so.

Sincerely,

Linda Birch
Personnel Manager

TO PRESIDENT OF COMPANY ADVISING
OF CORPORATE CONTRIBUTIONS FOR THE YEAR

TO : Lawrence M. Donovan
       President
FROM: Bradley T. Tower
SUBJ: CORPORATE CONTRIBUTIONS FOR 19——

I am attaching a list of programs that the Contributions Committee has approved for 19——, and we would like you to review this list.

If you have any questions or changes, please let me know. We will make distribution of the funds in January.

Attachment

SPONSORED PROGRAMS

CIVIC ACTIVITIES

Committee of '70
Crime Commission—Philadelphia
Fellowship Commission
League of Women Voters
National Conference of Christians &
  Jews
Old Philadelphia Development
  Corporation

MINORITY AFFAIRS

Wharton Community Education
  Program
Greater Philadelphia Develop. Corp.
Women's Way
NAACP
Phila. Council of Neighborhood Orgs.
OIC
Philadelphia Business Academy
Philadelphia Urban Coalition
Salvation Army
YWCA

CULTURAL ACTIVITIES

Channel 12
Drama Program—Philadelphia Schools
Pennsylvania Ballet
Philadelphia Museum of Art
Philadelphia Orchestra
Tiberlake Camp

CIVIC GROUPS

Anti-Defamation League
Pennsylvania Economy League
Pennsylvania Environment Council
Philadelphia Partnership

EDUCATION ACTIVITIES

Academy of Natural Sciences
Franklin Institute
Free Library of Philadelphia

ORGANIZED CHARITIES

American Cancer Society
Goodwill
Volunteers of America

YOUTH ACTIVITIES

Aspira
Boy Scouts of America
Junior Achievement
YMCA
PAL
Young Life

YOUTH

Pop Warner

EDUCATION

Philadelphia College
of Performing Arts

7

Letters Regarding
Policies and Procedures

Writing about personnel policies and procedures can be dangerous in several ways.

1. You run the risk of turning employees off, endangering morale, if you write policies in a "you will or else" tone. Employees like to feel they conform to policies and follow company procedures because it's right, not because the company stood over them with a whip.

2. If you are too laid-back in writing style, you might miss some important issues that can come back to haunt you if there is litigation. You need to find the happy medium of words and tone.

3. Some courts today are saying that employee handbooks and personnel policy manuals are employment contracts. It's a good idea to include a disclaimer clause in your handbook. The clause should state that the handbook should not be construed as a contract. Another employer protection is a statement that an employee can be terminated at the option of the company with no further obligation other than to pay wages already due the employee.

MANAGER'S TIPS FOR LETTERS ON
PERSONNEL POLICIES AND PROCEDURES

• It's a good idea when you write important letters regarding policies or procedures to ask another manager to review your letter and see what that manager feels about it before you send it.

• Write these letters in a personal style that eliminates the "you're in the Army now" syndrome.

Six Keys to Effective Letters on Personnel Policies

Key Element	*Policy Explanation*
Rapport	Your correspondence creates an aura of respect and concern for the receiver's feelings and desires.
Empathy	Good writers put themselves in the other person's place. The reader feels the writer understands the situation.
Personality	The writer expresses a personality. Is not boring and humorless.
Organization	Organization of the letter provides instant understanding of the message.
Clear, concise writing	Writer uses appropriate words and sentences to get the point across.
Editing	Writer reads the letter pretending to be the receiver. Edits for technical accuracy and for a total feeling from the letter.

Letters on personnel policies should give the employee a feeling of well-being.

REGARDING DRAFT OF EMPLOYEE HANDBOOK

Mr. Harold M. Schwendinger
Red Feather Coal Company
P.O. Box 620
Hanna, Wyoming 82327

Dear Harold:

A preliminary draft of the Red Feather Coal Company Employee Handbook is attached for your review. Copies have been furnished to Dick King and Tom Westgard. Revisions may be necessary after their review. Any revisions will be forwarded to you.

It seemed the only items not covered were:

Emergency Phone Calls
Employment of Relatives
Hand Tools

These policies could best be written by you after a decision has been made that these policies are needed.

It is my feeling that a policy on the employment of relatives should only restrict employment in the same department or direct reporting relationships, but a company-wide restriction is not practical for several reasons. The main reason is that in a small community, you don't staff a mine without hiring relatives.

The section I added on Equal Employment Opportunity is required by Sec. 6-2.21 OFCC Affirmative Action Guidelines pursuant to EO 11246.

If we can be of any further assistance, let me know. I would appreciate receiving several copies of the final handbook after it's printed.

Sincerely,

Eunice Schaeffer
Human Resources Director

REGARDING LATEST PERSONNEL PROCEDURES MANUAL BEING FURNISHED TO GENERAL MANAGER

Mr. Willard Kane
General Manager
Construction Materials Department
Allied Construction Company
Box 1143
Salt Lake City, Utah 84120

Dear Will:

Enclosed is your copy of the latest Personnel Procedures Manual. It is designed to be a "how to" guide that should answer most of the questions that arise concerning employment, discipline, terminations, salary increases, compensation, benefits, and training. Please ensure that the people involved in these areas review the book and have continued access to it.

If any of the procedures described in the manual cause problems or can be improved upon, we are happy to discuss alternatives if they can be worked out to our mutual benefit.

I look forward to seeing you on my next trip to Salt Lake City sometime during the first part of June. I'll call you when I have the exact date.

Sincerely,

Gene O. Hanson
Personnel Manager

TO DEPARTMENT HEADS
ENCLOSING SUPERVISOR'S HANDBOOK

TO: All Department Heads, Managers, and Supervisors

We are pleased to attach the revised pages for your Supervisor's Handbook.

The changes include an explanation regarding the "Birthday Off Holiday" in the Policies and Practices section, as well as a revised Life/Medical Rate Table and information on Dental Insurance in the Group Insurance Benefits portion of the handbook.

If you have any questions about these changes, please contact Personnel.

Sincerely,

Barbara L. Allen
Vice President
Personnel

REGARDING POLICY ON
PERSONAL LEAVE OF ABSENCE

Mr. Able L. Sinclair
General Manager
Food Service Industries, Inc.
Post Office Box 2000
Omaha, Nebraska 68121

Dear Mr. Sinclair:

Attached is a revised Personal Leave of Absence Request form. This is the form that should be given to employees when they express an interest in requesting a leave of absence.

Since the status of benefits is relatively complex, please ask all employees with questions about a leave of absence to call me on extension 3692.

Sincerely,

Linda P. Mason
Personnel Manager

Attachment

Personal Leave of Absence Request

Name:	Last	First	Middle	Date of Request
Address:	Street	City	State	Zip Code
Hire Date		Social Security Number		Phone Number Home _____ Work _____
Effective Date		Date of Return		Department

Briefly explain the reason for your request _____

While you are on a Personal Leave of Absence, all Company benefits will be suspended; however, you may convert your medical and life insurance coverage to an individual policy if your application is received by the insurance company within 31 days. If you would like to take advantage of this option or would like more information, please check one of the boxes below. Upon return, the date of the next scheduled merit increase will be extended by the length of the leave of absence.

Failure to return to work on the expected date of return will result in a voluntary termination unless you have received a <u>written</u> extension. The effective date of the termination will be the last day actually worked.

<u>Insurance Option</u>

☐ No Interest

☐ Please ask the insurance company to send policy options and enrollment information.

_____

Employee Signature   Date

Approved:

Recommended:

_____   _____
Supervisor   Date   Department Manager Date

```
┌─────────────────────────────────────────────────────────────────────┐
│ Reviewed by:                                                          │
│                                                                       │
│ _____              _____  │
│ Personnel Department                     Date                         │
│                                                                       │
└─────────────────────────────────────────────────────────────────────┘
```

REGARDING PERSONAL TIME OFF
SELL BACK POLICY

TO: All Employees: Medical Center & Affiliates
FROM: Phyllis J. Engen
      Corporate Human Resources Director
SUBJ: PTO (PERSONAL TIME OFF) SELL BACK POLICY

We have made a major change in our PTO Sell Back Policy. These changes will give you the opportunity to sell back excess PTO hours twice a year. Under the new policy you will be able to sell back your PTO at <u>100% of current wage value rather than the reduced rate.</u> The new procedure for PTO sell back, effective July 1st, is as follows:

1. <u>It is your responsibility to request the PTO sell back</u> prior to your anniversary date and/or during the first week of December. Management employees on the matrix may sell back prior to their matrix review date. Your PTO accumulation is shown on each paycheck stub. Make your intentions known to your Human Resources Department.

2. All hours over 40 may be sold back, provided you have used hours in accordance with the following schedule:

Hours must be taken:	If accrual is:
128 hours	24 days per anniversary year
140 hours	29 days per anniversary year
160 hours	34 days per anniversary year

3. If you have used the hours as outlined in the schedule above in the previous 12 months and have a balance of more than 40 hours, any additional hours over 40 <u>may be sold back at 100% of current wage value.</u>

4. All hours over 448 will automatically be sold back prior to your anniversary date and the first week in December in accordance with the following schedule:

Under 5 years service	50% of wage value
5 through 14 years service	75% of wage value
15 years or more service	100% of wage value

This policy generously liberalizes our PTO program. Not only does it provide employees with an opportunity to sell back their PTO at a higher rate and on a more frequent basis, it also reduces the Medical Center's liability of earned but unpaid PTO.

REGARDING DELEGATION OF AUTHORITY

TO: All Executives

FROM: William T. Titus, President

SUBJ: DELEGATION OF AUTHORITY

Reserved authority of the Office of the President, Construction Sources Company, is hereby delegated to:

Eugene M. Greene, senior vice-president

while I am away from the office, August 25 through August 29.

POLICY ON WITHHOLDING INCOME TAX

Mr. Harold J. Cooper
6230 Roberts Street
Casper, Wyoming 82601

Dear Harold:

L. Clarkson, manager, Tax and Treasury, has advised that two primary conditions must be met before the company can stop withholding Colorado Income Tax from your check. First, you must not be performing employment services in Colorado, and second, you must be a bona fide resident of Wyoming.

Please send me a statement verifying that Wyoming is your state of residence. Upon receipt, we will honor your request and cease Colorado withholding until you return to Colorado to live.

Sincerely,

Laurence Wright
Personnel Manager

LETTER ENCLOSING COPIES OF EQUAL EMPLOYMENT OPPORTUNITY POLICIES AND PROCEDURES

Ms. Julie B. Aragon
Director of Employee Development
NERCO, Inc.
111 S.W. Columbia
Portland, Oregon 97201

Dear Julie:

I enjoyed seeing you again at the Mountain States Employers Council Conference last week. I am enclosing copies of the personnel policies you requested regarding sexual harassment. The three policies that cover this subject are:

Equal Employment Opportunity
Equal Opportunity Complaint Procedures
Employee Complaint Procedures

We have a separate departmental procedure for handling complaints. We record the complaint and the findings, and assign the responsibility for investigation to our EEO coordinator. It is the coordinator's responsibility to follow through to ensure that the complaint is resolved satisfactorily.

I hope this information is of some assistance. If you have any questions please give me a call.

Sincerely,

Mary F. Cook
Director, Employee Relations

DISCUSSION MEMO FOR EXECUTIVE STAFF MEETING ON FLEXTIME

TO:	Executive Staff Members
FROM:	Mary F. Cook
	Director of Employee Relations
SUBJ:	FLEXTIME

We've had several requests from employees over the past 12 months to consider flextime as an alternative work schedule. Recently, discussions have centered around the longer drive some employees will have when we move to our new home office facility, and the idea that flextime would be one alternative to heavy traffic or commuting problems.

A brief review of the flextime concept might be in order.

The Flextime Concept

As indicated by the attached chart, a fixed workday usually requires employees to be on the job between 8:00 A.M. and 5:00 P.M., with an hour off for lunch. A day with flexible work hours lets the employees report at any point in their first flextime period and leave at any point in the second period, provided they work the required number of hours for the week. During "core time," everyone is working or at lunch—as they would be on a fixed workday.

During the course of a week, employees are expected to work 40 hours, with overtime accumulating beyond that point. On any given day, however, they might work from five to ten hours.

Some Flextime Advantages Reported in a Recent Survey
Conducted by the WALL STREET JOURNAL

- Higher efficiency because employees work when they are most productive.
- Less likelihood that workers will call in sick rather than ask permission to arrive late or leave early.

- Employees can reduce fatigue by avoiding rush-hour traffic.
- Absenteeism and turnovers decrease because workers find it easier to combine afternoon child-care duties with the demands of a job.

Most Disadvantages Are Minor

One drawback of a flextime system might be that not all departments can participate. Professional, technical, and office staffs working on individual projects are the easiest to accommodate. Production operations, such as Sample Plant or Data Processing, may require interdependence. In some operations, the system works best if the entire group agrees to arrive and leave at the same time. These disadvantages are not insurmountable, since some departments can work on fixed hours and others on flextime.

Transportation could be a problem, since employees will tend to arrive individually rather than in carpools. Since the building will be open longer, we may also incur higher expenses for light and heat. Usually, the costs are outweighed by the benefits of a flextime system. However, one drawback—which can be more serious—involves monitoring the daily schedules of employees. If managers "manage" the system well, it works well.

Time Recording Is Essential

When you use a flexible schedule, it is impossible to keep track of employees' work hours without a recording system. Our regular Exception Reports should take care of this.

The administrative costs are usually low in comparison to the benefits.

Testing the Idea

One way to know if a flexible schedule will work well in our company is to try a short-term experiment. Bill Zabriskie is experimenting with flextime in his group now. We will follow up with Bill to see how his test is working, and at the end of the trial period, survey his and the employees' reactions.

I suggest that we try flextime throughout the company on a six-month trial basis. Once we start a program of this type, it's difficult to back out of it, but it's much easier if it is understood from the beginning that it is a pilot program.

One way to ensure that everyone understands it is a pilot program is to assign an employee committee to help monitor progress and the pros and cons as they evolve.

Before management introduces flextime, we should be certain flextime will be consistent with our objectives, leadership styles, company policies, and organizational structure. Some questions we should answer before considering flextime are:

- Does the concept of flextime have application to ROC?
- Does it appear to offer solutions to scheduling problems if there are any?
- Is the size of our work force sufficiently large, or the workload of a nature that flextime could work?
- Are there positions that could not be converted to flextime?
- What types of problems could result from the restriction on some positions?

• Has a careful examination of workload and interface factors been done?
• Are our managers capable of managing flextime successfully?

Another alternative to flextime is altering the fixed work schedules to, say, 7:00 A.M. to 4:00 P.M. during the summer to avoid traffic problems and to allow employees more daylight time with their families.

Attached is a proposed draft of a memo and an Employee Survey. I'd appreciate your reviewing these documents and returning them to me with your comments by December 30th.

TO MANAGERS REGARDING REVISION OF THE COMPANY JOB BID PROGRAM

    TO: All Supervisors and Managers
FROM: Nancy Larson
           Personnel Manager
  SUBJ: REVISION OF THE JOB BID PROGRAM

The Employment section of the Personnel Department is in the process of studying and revising the current job bid program.

It is our desire to make the program more efficient for the managers of the various divisions, the people in the Personnel Division whose responsibility it is to administer it, and for employees who use the program. There is also a need on the part of the Personnel Department to ensure uniform procedures whereby all employees from Grade B up through Supervisor have the capability to advance within the organization.

Your comments and constructive recommendations for improvement of the job bid program are solicited.

Attached are the proposed revisions and pertinent exhibits. We would appreciate your reviewing, commenting on, and returning the revisions to us by July 25.

Please contact Edwin Greene on ext. 2840 if you have any questions about this project. Ed is in charge of the bid program revisions and will welcome your participation and involvement.

TO EMPLOYEES FURNISHING REVISED JOB BID PROCEDURES

    TO: All Employees
FROM: Nancy Larson
           Personnel Manager
  SUBJ: EMPLOYEE BID PROGRAM REVISIONS
         EFFECTIVE AUGUST 1, 19——

During the past few months, the Employment section of the Personnel Department has investigated, compiled, and analyzed information pertaining to the Employee

Bid Program. Blue Cross of Connecticut, local companies with similar programs, as well as managers, supervisors, and employees of the Colorado Plans were sources of information.

The study brought to light some inadequacies in the present system. We hope to eliminate those inadequacies during a six-month trial period in which the revised bid program will be implemented.

The purpose of the Employee Bid Program is to establish a uniform system of posting available opportunities to benefit all employees. Please keep this in mind as you review the following changes:

1. All employees are eligible to bid, with the exception of:
   a. Individuals on probationary period. Probationary period is three months for wage employees and six months for salaried. This includes employee-initiated transfers, demotions, or promotions unless in the best interests of the company.
   b. Employees currently on a documented disciplinary action for poor performance, attendance, etc.
2. All job openings at grade B level or above, including salaried positions up to manager, will be posted on the bid board. The current policy is to post grade C level and above.
3. Bids will be posted for five working days. Employees should submit their bids within this time period.
4. The Employment section of the Personnel Department will screen the bids and forward them to the receiving manager. If a bid is not accepted, it will be returned to the employee with an explanation.
5. Interviews should not last beyond the tenth working day after the initial posting.
6. The receiving department should not make a decision before the fifth day after the bid is posted.
7. The receiving manager should return the signed bid form, with comments, to the Employment section within ten working days after the position has been filled. It is important that the manager's comments include:
   a. Specific reasons why the candidate was or was not chosen.
   b. Positive statements that will encourage the employee to bid again.
   c. Specific reasons why another candidate was chosen.
8. Job titles of available positions will be listed weekly in the Newsletter.
9. The new section of the bid bulletin board will include:
   a. Regulations
   b. Wage grades
   c. Recent recipients of posted jobs
   d. Current week's bids
10. Changes have been made in the Employee Bid Form No. 70010 and the Requisition Form No. 70036 to allow for more detailed and relevant information.

<u>Weekly Schedule</u>

<u>Monday morning</u>—Posting of current job opportunities on the bid board and a list of job titles in the Newsletter.

<u>Thursday noon</u>—Deadline for submitting bids to Personnel for posting and for inclusion in the Newsletter.

<u>Friday at 4:00 P.M.</u>—Remove bids from the bulletin board. No more bids received from employees.

Additional information on the revised bid system will be appearing in the Newsletter.

If you have any questions or comments pertaining to the revised Bid Program, please direct them to Ed Greene on ext. 2840. Ed has been responsible for preparing revisions to the bid program and will welcome your participation.

HUMAN RESOURCES COMPUTER SYSTEM
(HRS) ON-LINE

TO: M. F. Johnson
FROM: R. T. Perez
SUBJ: HUMAN RESOURCES SYSTEM (HRS) ON-LINE

We have worked with Business Systems since 19——, developing a combination of hardware and software that would allow updating the computerized Human Resources System (HRS) to utilize an on-line desktop terminal in Employee Relations. Current practice requires punching cards and delivering them to Data Processing for input.

Utilizing the on-line terminal has several advantages, with the only identified disadvantage being the cost of implementation and ongoing operation.

ADVANTAGES

- With the built-in edit feature, data entry errors can be caught and eliminated prior to the information entering the system. Today, errors are shown on an edit report following acceptance of the information. They must be researched and then corrected by punching and submitting additional key punch cards.
- Timeliness of information will be improved because changes can be made on a daily basis. This is not presently feasible because of logistical and scheduling difficulties.
  Delays in inputting information from other locations is significant because the HRS profiles must be mailed to Denver before being entered into the computer. Going on-line now will provide the future option of placing terminals at remote locations to allow rapid records update.
- Moving on-line now for purposes of data input will be the initial step toward acquiring the capability to conduct timely searches utilizing the same hardware. Working with our system, the Data Processing Department can gain expertise in building retrieval capability into other systems that will be coming on-line in the next year.

Discussions with Computer Science, Inc. have taken place, and the necessary application software can be purchased. The cost of the system software that is required for ongoing operation aggregates approximately $_____ per month. Other installation and operational considerations are also outlined in that memo.

With the support of the Advisory Committee, we can install the system in 19——. By committing to purchase the package as soon as possible, we may realize the several benefits described in the Contract Options section of the attached Appendix A. In summary, it provides for a possible $_____ discount and a price freeze if we also purchase their Payroll System.

I recommend that the necessary approvals be sought so that we can be on-line, with our staff trained, prior to the heavy workload that will accompany the 19—— wage and salary increases.

FURNISHING COPY OF LICENSE AGREEMENT FOR AN ON-LINE HUMAN RESOURCES COMPUTER SYSTEM

TO: Ralph Fraser
FROM: Colleen Boyd
SUBJ: HUMAN RESOURCES SYSTEM (HRS) ON-LINE PACKAGE

Ralph, I am attaching a copy of the License Agreement for the HRS on-line system.

It was necessary that we execute this agreement prior to January 1 in order to get a 40 percent discount on the system. Our cost was $9,900; after January 1st, it would have been $16,500. This agreement was on your desk for several days while you were out of the office. After having Lloyd Reid, Bill Johns, Steve Sota, et al. review and approve the agreement, I asked Larry Welch to sign it so we could get it in the mail.

I had budgeted and planned for this system, so there was nothing new or unexpected. I understand that Rick and Bill had also planned for its installation, so I felt there were no surprises. But I wanted to let you know what I had done, and that we did get "under the wire" on the lower price.

8

Letters to Various Government and Regulatory Agencies

In today's working environment, a personnel manager frequently has the need to correspond with city, state, or federal government agencies. There is always a question of how best to communicate the message, how best to set a tone either for taking a justifiable stand or for conciliation and agreement. A tone of cooperation and openness is always the best idea. Many times, when writing to a government agency, you find yourself corresponding with a computer, so it's important to include in your correspondence references to case numbers, correspondence dates, formal names, and any other type of identification used by the agency.

MANAGER'S TIPS FOR REGULATORY CORRESPONDENCE

- Regulatory correspondence is just like any other business correspondence. Keep it short, simple, to the point, with a businesslike tone, but not pompous or curt.
- Letters to regulatory agencies should include more references to specific data, lists of items, numbers, and citations, listing specific regulations or court findings.
- Letters to employees regarding EEO charges, OSHA charges, or any other regulatory problems should state the facts and the company's position, but not condemn or blame anyone, including the agency, for a problem, if one exists.

SEXUAL BIAS AND RACIAL STEREOTYPES IN ORGANIZATIONAL COMMUNICATION

Equal Opportunity has been around a long time. It is a basic human right, and organizational communicators have a special responsibility to fulfill affirmative action requirements by writing in a non-sexist, non-discriminatory manner. Equally important is an ability to use their unique roles in business to counsel management and to help set the tone for the whole organization.

Today's workers are more aware and knowledgeable regarding stereotypes and bias, and the human resource manager needs a keen awareness of writing style.

The International Association of Business Communicators has published a guidebook, entitled *Without Bias: A Guidebook for Non-Discriminatory Communication*. It provides an excellent review of racial and ethnic stereotypes and how to avoid them in writing. The book also provides information on sexual bias in communication and how to eliminate it.

For example, the guidebook provides the following test for racial stereotypes:

Avoid Using Qualifiers That Reinforce Racial and Ethnic Stereotypes. A qualifier is information added that suggests an exception to the rule. Example: An account of a company event read, "The intelligent black students were guests as part of an orientation program...." Under what circumstances would someone write, "The intelligent white students..."?

To determine whether or not a qualifier has been used, try this test: Imagine the sentence with the word "white" in place of "black," or substitute an Anglo surname for a Chicano or Asian one. Bias is subtle. The more deeply it has been assimilated, the more difficult it is to eliminate.

The guidebook also provides the following tests for sexual bias:

The most subtle form of sexism is the omission of women in references that take in humanity at large. The word "man" has been used in describing the male gender and in describing humanity as a whole, a practice potentially offensive to the communicator's audience.

Include all people in general references by substituting asexual words and phrases for man-words.

NO	YES
mankind	people, humanity, human beings, human race
man-made	synthetic, artificial, constructed, manufactured, of human origin
manpower	human resources, human energy, workers, workforce
gentleman's agreement	informal agreement or contract

The lack of a generic singular pronoun in the English language causes many editorial headaches. The continued use of the phrase "he or she" can make writing difficult to read. Stubborn insistence that the pronouns "he," "him," and "his" stand for all people can also create problems. Consider this sentence taken from a group insurance brochure: "If the employee becomes pregnant while covered under this policy, he will be entitled to..."

Consider various alternatives when using pronouns; reword the sentence to eliminate unnecessary gender pronouns, or recase into the plural.

TO EEOC REPRESENTATIVE REGARDING SEX DISCRIMINATION CHARGE FILED BY FORMER EMPLOYEE

Mr. Robert L. Baker
Commission Representative
Equal Employment Opportunity Commission
Denver District Office
1531 Stout Street
Denver, Colorado 80202

     Re: Charge No. 0132400T
        Charging Party: Ms. Linda T. Brown

Dear Mr. Baker:

Following is Western Energy Company's response to your questions regardng the sex discrimination charge of Ms. Linda T. Brown:

Western Energy Company Position Statement

1. On April 29, 19———, Ms. Brown's employment was terminated due to company-wide reduction in force.

    a. Ms. Brown's date of hire was May 1, 19———.

    b. Western Energy Company had 647 employees as of September 1, 19———.

    c. At the time of the reduction in force, sixteen persons were employed in the Accounting Department. Of the sixteen persons employed, one was the department manager, three were supervisors, six were professionals, and six were office and clerical employees.

2. On April 26, 19———, Mr. Robert L. Johnson, manager of the Land Department, telephoned Ms. Brown at the Houston office and informed her that she was going to be terminated effective April 29, 19———. She was told that she would receive severance pay and vacation pay, and that her medical benefits would be continued for an additional 30 days after termination.

Mr. Lawrence Fey, vice-president of Human Resources, sent a letter to each affected employee confirming the termination and outlining the pay and benefits to be received. This letter was mailed on April 26.

3. Ms. Brown was not terminated because of her sex. She was terminated because her level of performance was unsatisfactory, which was in accordance with the criteria established for the reduction in force. The criteria for termination are listed below in order of priority.

    • Employees in jobs identified as nonessential
    • Employee's individual job performance
    • Less senior employees

Ms. Brown was not offered reassignment because her level of performance was not up to the required standard as evidenced by her past performance appraisals. There were no open positions in her job classification in any of our other offices.

4. On May 10, 19——, Ms. Brown was given the opportunity to appeal her dismissal in accordance with company personnel policy No. E-7. Ms. Brown did discuss her termination with Mr. Kenneth R. Green, vice-president of the Accounting Department, who is Mr. Johnson's immediate supervisor. Mr. Green suggested that he, Mr. Johnson, and Ms. Brown meet to discuss the termination. Ms. Brown declined, saying that she would call later to set a time for a meeting. Ms. Brown did not call again for a meeting.

Western Energy Company feels there is no basis for Ms. Brown's charge of sex discrimination. Her termination was justified and was in accordance with the reduction in force criteria the company established.

If you have further questions, please give me a call.

Sincerely,

Mary F. Cook
Director, Human Resources

TO <u>OSHA</u> ADMINISTRATOR REGARDING SAFETY CITATION

Donald D. Owsley, Administrator
  State of Wyoming
Occupational Health & Safety Department
200 East 8th Avenue
Cheyenne, Wyoming 82002

     Re: Citation No. 99981/M009978
         Date of Citation: March 18, 19——

Dear Mr. Owsley:

By means of this letter I wish to notify you that our subsidiary, Champlin Petroleum Company, contests the alleged violation, the specified abatement period, and the penalty proposed in the Notice of Violation, Citation No. 99981/M009978, dated March 18, 19——.

Additionally, Champlin Petroleum Company requests that an informal conference be set in this matter as soon as possible.

Sincerely,

Mary H. Henderson
Legal Assistant
Natural Resources

TO EEOC REGARDING
AGE DISCRIMINATION CHARGE

Ms. Mary Beekman
U.S. EEOC
St. Louis District Office
84 N. Hampden
St. Louis, Missouri 63137

Re: Case No. 111–11–111

Dear Ms. Beekman:

In response to your letter of October 2, 19———, Manville Corporation presents the following information for your review in the age discrimination charge filed by Sam Jones:

Allegation	Company Response
1. I was the only plant maintenance engineer over 50 years old who was terminated.	Mr. Jones chose to retire; he was not terminated. Four other engineers over 50 are still working for the company.
2. My retirement pay is $40 a month less than the estimates I received four months ago.	The benefits calculation made in January of 19——— included a tentative 5 percent salary increase for all employees that management subsequently did not grant. The figures given Mr. Jones were preliminary estimates subject to final verification on the date he actually retired.
3. My performance was acceptable, but I was not offered another job.	Since Mr. Jones voluntarily elected retirement, this allegation is not relevant.

The company denies that any act of discrimination occurred in Mr. Jones's decision to retire. If you need further information, please call me.

Cordially,

Patty Ptacek
Manager, Employee Relations

**TO EEOC REGARDING
CHARGE OF AGE DISCRIMINATION**

Mr. Paul Jones
Equal Opportunity Specialist
Equal Employment Opportunity Commission
Denver District Office
One Stout Street
Denver, Colorado 80200

> Re: Charge No. 060602222
> Charging Party: John Brown

Dear Mr. Jones:

Enclosed is the information that you requested concerning the above-referenced charge of age discrimination.

Exhibit 1:   Mr. Brown's personnel file, employment application, and performance appraisals.

Exhibit 2:   A copy of the Company's policy concerning work rules. These rules were printed in the Handbook given to Mr. Brown at the time he was hired.

Exhibit 2a: A copy of the Company's policy concerning Disciplinary Action and Warning Notices. This policy is found in the Company's Personnel Policy Manual.

Exhibit 2b: A copy of the Company's Policy on Procedures and Causes for Termination. This policy is also found in the Personnel Policy Manual.

Exhibit 3:   The names, ages, position titles, and dates of hire of the employees in the unit where Mr. Brown worked.

Exhibit 4:   Dates of birth of the department manager and supervisor of Mr. Brown's department.

Exhibit 5:   Name, date of birth, and date of hire of Mr. Brown's replacement.

Exhibit 6:   Memorandum reporting the verbal reprimand Mr. Brown received from his supervisor on June 10, 19——.

Exhibit 6a: Copy of the written reprimand Mr. Brown received from his supervisor on July 10, 19——.

Exhibit 6b: Copy of Mr. Brown's response to the written reprimand he received on July 10, 19——.

Exhibit 6c: Memorandum reporting Mr. Brown's termination from the Company on July 31, 19——.

I have enclosed all relevant information. If you have any questions, please feel free to call me.

Sincerely,

Myrna D. Mourning
Affirmative Action Officer

TO <u>EEOC</u> IN RESPONSE TO INTERROGATORIES ON A CHARGE OF SEX DISCRIMINATION

Mr. William Smith
Commission Representative
Equal Employment Opportunity Commission
Denver District Office
One Stout Street
Denver, Colorado 80200

> Re: Charge No. 071711800
> Charging Party: Ms. Jane Doe

Dear Mr. Smith:

Enclosed is the Company's response to the sex discrimination charge filed by Ms. Jane Doe.

The Company's Position Statement

I. On July 1, 19——, Ms. Doe's employment was terminated due to a company-wide reduction in force.

   a. Ms. Doe's date of hire was June 1, 19——.

   b. The Company had 500 employees as of September 1, 19——.

   c. At the time of the reduction in force, fifteen persons were employed in Ms. Doe's former department. Of the fifteen persons employed, one was the department manager, two were supervisors, six were professionals, and another six were office and clerical employees.

II. On June 28, 19——, the department manager telephoned Ms. Doe at the Wyoming office and informed her that she had been selected for termination, effective July 1, 19——. On July 1, 19——, the vice-president of the Personnel Department sent each affected employee a letter that confirmed his or her termination due to a reduction in force.

In addition, the letter contained information pertaining to the terminating employee's benefits—i.e., insurance coverage, termination pay, severance pay, and unused and accrued vacation pay. Also included in the letter was information regarding the job counseling and résumé preparation service that the Company would be providing to affected employees (refer to Exhibit 1).

III. Ms. Doe was not terminated because of her sex. She was terminated because her level of performance was unsatisfactory, in accordance with the Reduction in Force criteria (refer to Exhibit 2). The criteria used to determine which employees would be terminated are listed below in order of priority:

   a. Employees in jobs identified as nonessential.

   b. Employees' individual performance levels.

   c. Less senior employees.

Ms. Doe was not offered reassignment because her level of performance was not up to the required standard. She was the only supervisor in the Wyoming office, and since there were no vacant supervisory positions in the Colorado office, there was nothing available for her.

Performance was one criterion used for selecting employees for termination. Seniority was also a criterion, but only if the performance of two employees was equal. This did not apply to Ms. Doe's particular situation. Any Company supervisor, male or female, with performance similar to Ms. Doe's would have been disciplined.

Ms. Doe's manager did not state that, as a woman, Ms. Doe should not have reprimanded the male consultants who reported to her, and he had no such attitude.

Seniority, as stated above, was the least important of the three criteria considered in the reduction in force.

IV. On August 2, 19——, Ms. Doe was given the opportunity to appeal her dismissal in accordance with the Company Personnel Policies Nos. E3 and E7, outlining the Company's complaint resolution procedures (refer to Exhibits 3 and 3A). Ms. Doe discussed the situation of termination with the vice-president of the department, and he agreed to meet with her and the manager. The meeting was arranged; when Ms. Doe was asked to attend, she said that she "could not meet at that time," and indicated that she would like to reschedule for a later date. She never called to set up a suitable time, and no such meeting ever occurred.

The Questionnaire

1. The Company's position statement appears above.
2. Ms. Doe was terminated on July 1, 19—— because of a Company-wide reduction in force. On June 28, 19——, the department manager informed Ms. Doe that she would be terminated on July 1, 19——. Ms. Doe was selected for termination because of her unsatisfactory level of performance.
3. Ms. Doe had more seniority than Messrs. Grey, Jones, and White. She was not offered reassignment because of her unsatisfactory performance.
4. The reduction in force policy was established by senior management of the Company. No written policy has been issued to employees.
5. The charging party was terminated solely in accordance with the reduction in force criteria.
6. All employees affected by the reduction in force are listed by name, sex, job title, date of hire, and department in Exhibit 4. Seniority date is not applicable at the Company.

There is no basis for Ms. Doe's charge of sex discrimination. Her termination was justified and in accordance with the reduction in force criteria.

If you have further questions, please feel free to telephone me.

Sincerely,

Myrna D. Mourning
Affirmative Action Officer

RESPONSE TO EEOC CHARGE ON A PERSON THAT WAS EMPLOYED BY A GUARD SERVICE UNDER CONTRACT TO THE COMPANY

Mr. Joe Rosenberg
Equal Employment Opportunity Commission
1845 Sherman Street, 2nd Floor
Denver, Colorado 80203

> Re: Charge No. 0613247
> Charging Party: Lester L. Hynes

Dear Mr. Rosenberg:

Relative to our telephone conversation yesterday, I am providing the information you requested regarding Charge No. 0613247, concerning Lester L. Hynes. Mr. Hynes was not an employee of Sorenson Mfg. Co. He was employed by Wells-Lang Security Guard Service and worked as a contract guard at our facility.

The Sorenson Mfg. Co. procedures regarding contract services preclude our taking any personnel or termination action with contractors' employees.

If you need further assistance in this matter, please do not hesitate to call me.

Sincerely,

Edgar Whitelock
Personnel Manager

TO FAIR EMPLOYMENT COMMISSION REGARDING STATE CIVIL RIGHTS CHARGE

Bob Warburton
Compliance Officer
Wyoming Fair Employment Commission
Department of Labor and Statistics
P.O. Box 1134
Casper, Wyoming 82602

> Re: Jane T. Doe vs. Bear Creek Uranium Company;
> Wyoming Fair Employment Commission #888-1983

Dear Mr. Warburton:

This office represents our affiliate Bear Creek Uranium Company, Employer-Defendant, herein. Mr. Anthony M. Justice, Employee Relations Manager, Bear Creek Uranium Company, has asked us to respond to your letter of April 8 19——, concerning referenced complaint.

Bear Creek Uranium Company is prepared to cooperate with you in the required investigation and at an appropriate time will share with you results and impressions gained from its internal review of the complaint.

I would suggest that you advise this office of the date, time and place of the informal conference, which we have agreed may be at your convenience.

If you have any questions regarding any of the forgoing, please advise.

Sincerely,

Mary H. Henderson
Legal Assistant
Natural Resources

TO STATE EMPLOYMENT SECURITY COMMISSION REGARDING CLAIM FOR UNEMPLOYMENT INSURANCE

Theodore D. Maras
Appeals Examiner
Employment Security Commission
 of Wyoming
P.O. Box 2760
Casper, Wyoming 82602

> Re: In the matter of the Claim for Unemployment Insurance by John R. Doe, Claimant, vs. Stansbury Coal Company, Employer-Appellant; Appeal No, 99-XX-83; before the Employment Security Commission of the State of Wyoming

Dear Mr. Maras:

This office represents Stansbury Coal Company, Employer-Appellant, in referenced claim, and on its behalf submits the following pertinent facts for consideration at the hearing on appeal:

I. <u>Grounds for Discharge.</u>

Claimant was discharged on April 1, 19——, for gross misconduct.

II. <u>Position of Stansbury Coal Company.</u>

The grounds for discharge specified in Paragraph I above constitute the sole and only reason for Claimant's discharge and Claimant is not entitled therefore to unemployment compensation benefits by virtue of §27-3-106(c), W.S. 1977, the Wyoming Employment Security Act, which provides as follows:

- **§27-3-106(c). Disqualifications for benefits.**
  (c) An individual shall be disqualified for benefits and shall forfeit all accrued benefits if he has been discharged from his most recent work for misconduct connected with his work, fraud, or receipt of disqualifying income. [emphasis supplied]

III. Claimant's Employment History and Employer's Comments Respecting Reason for Claimant's Separation from Employment.

Claimant was hired as diesel mechanic on August 5, 19—— at the rate of $700.00 per week. His job performance and work record were relatively problem-free. However, on April 1, 19——, claimant was caught stealing company property (money from the office cash box) and was immediately terminated by his supervisor, Janice B. Foreman, for gross misconduct. Claimant admitted his wrongdoing to Mrs. Foreman at the time the incident took place, which was during claimant's regular shift, while he was on duty.

It is common knowledge and a work rule at the mine that such actions by employees are considered serious misconduct and may result in disciplinary action up to and including discharge. The Stansbury Employee Handbook provides:

- **Work Rules.**
  Rules are for the benefit and protection of both the employee and employer and must be enforced. Any of the following actions by an employee are considered serious misconduct and may result in disciplinary action up to and including discharge.
  …2. Vandalism, careless destruction of Company property, or theft of property belonging to the Company or a fellow employee will not be tolerated." [emphasis supplied]

Claimant was regarded in all respects as a seasoned employee familiar with Company work rules and policies.

IV. Conclusion.

Based on the forgoing, it is appellant's position that due to Claimant's own dishonest actions, his involuntary termination for gross misconduct arose, and appellant therefore respectfully requests that this Claim be dismissed as to Stansbury Coal Company and that the Commission find that Mr. Doe was discharged for gross misconduct and is therefore not entitled to unemployment compensation benefits pursuant to §27-3-106(c), W.S. 1977.

Respectfully,

Mary H. Henderson
Legal Assistant
Natural Resources

**TO OFFICE OF FEDERAL
CONTRACT COMPLIANCE PROGRAMS
REGARDING COMPLIANCE REVIEW**

Mr. Malcolm Holliman
Acting Denver Area Director
U.S. Department of Labor
Employment Standards Administration
Office of Federal Contract Compliance Programs
2500 Curtis Street
Denver, Colorado 80205

Dear Mr. Holliman:

In compliance with our equal employment opportunity obligations under Executive
Order 11246, as amended, under Section 503 of the Rehabilitation Act of 1973, as
amended, and under Section 402 of the Vietnam Era Veterans Readjustment
Assistance Act of 1974, we are submitting the following information and exhibits in
response to your request dated August 16, 19——:

Exhibit A   EEO-1 forms for the years 19——, 19——, and 19——.

Exhibit B   Work force analysis for January 1, 19——.

Exhibit C   Progression line charts as of January 1, 19——.

Exhibit D   19—— job group and availability analysis.

Exhibit E   Goals and timetable charts for 19—— and 19——.

Exhibit F   Analysis of our selection process.

Exhibit G   Analysis of promotions for 19—— and 19——.

Exhibit H   Analysis of terminations for 19—— and 19——.

Exhibit I   Affirmative Action Plan for Disabled and Veterans.

These exhibits should provide you with all the information you seek. However, if
we can furnish further information and answer questions that come up in your
review, please give us a call.

Sincerely,

Mary F. Cook
Director of Human Resources

TO VICE-PRESIDENT REGARDING
LETTER FROM OFFICE OF FEDERAL CONTRACT
COMPLIANCE PROGRAMS

Mr. James C. Haddock
Vice-President, Law Department
Houston Oil Company
Box C-330
Houston, Texas 77041

Dear Jim:

Attached for your information is a letter from the Office of Federal Contract
Compliance asking us to furnish them with a great deal of information on our
company. Because the information requested must be obtained from both the
Human Resources and the Law Departments, there will need to be a joint effort in
finalizing the response.

I would appreciate it if you would review the OFCCP letter and give me a call to
arrange a meeting at your earliest convenience. The OFCCP requested we furnish
the information within the next thirty days.

Sincerely,

William C. Mauch
Director
Human Resources

TO PRESIDENT OF COMPANY ADVISING
THAT A COMPLIANCE REVIEW
BY THE <u>OFCCP</u> HAS BEEN COMPLETED

Mr. Glen T. Jackson
President
Oil Properties Corporation
777 Seventeenth Street
Denver, Colorado 80202

Dear Mr. Jackson:

The OFCCP compliance review of our company's Equal Employment Opportunity
policies and practices has been completed.

The OFCCP found no deficiencies in our Affirmative Action program. The
program was therefore accepted.

This determination does not preclude a subsequent finding of noncompliance should we deviate substantially from the commitments set forth in the approved Affirmative Action program. This is good news, however, and I want to take this opportunity to compliment the Personnel Department staff for the fine job they have done with a very significant record-keeping job!

Sincerely,

Joanne Greystone
Personnel Director

TO VICE-PRESIDENT REVIEWING AFFIRMATIVE ACTION PROGRESS OF THE COMPANY

Mr. Wilson F. Jones
Vice-President
Jones-Schindler Corporation
1000 Highway 25
Colorado Springs, Colorado 80905

Dear Bill:

I have recently reviewed the Affirmative Action progress that was achieved by the Operating Companies and Corporate Headquarters in 19——. We are pleased to note that progress has been made in achieving our overall Affirmative Action projections within the Corporation. Despite this progress, we must continue our Affirmative Action efforts in 19——, especially as they relate to our managerial and professional level positions.

Attached is a copy of the Corporate Headquarters bulletin from the chairman that was sent to all Corporate employees, reaffirming the Corporation's policy on Equal Employment Opportunity. I would ask that you prepare a similar communication reaffirming our overall policy for your employees.

I am confident that with your continued efforts we will make progress toward achieving our goals during 19——.

Sincerely,

William A. Loggins
President

TO U.S. DEPARTMENT OF LABOR, OFFICE OF FEDERAL CONTRACT COMPLIANCE PROGRAMS REGARDING MINORITY VENDOR PROGRAM

Ms. Ann Occhino
U.S. Department of Labor
Employment Standards Administration
Office of Federal Contract
   Compliance Programs
2500 Curtis Street, Suite 100
Denver, Colorado 80205

Dear Ms. Occhino:

Our second quarter Minority Vendor Report just arrived, and I am sending you a copy as you requested.

We are pleased with the progress we are making this year. I expect this progress to continue throughout the remainder of 19——.

Sincerely,

Stanley Dalton
Personnel Director

TO SUPERVISORS REGARDING SEXUAL HARASSMENT POLICY

To All Supervisors:

The subject of sexual harassment continues to be widely discussed by the mass communication media. It is often a misunderstood, difficult, and uncomfortable issue for supervisors and employees alike. As a result, discussion of it is often greeted with smiles and jokes. This is, however, a very serious subject. The statutory law is in place and legal precedent is developing in the area, which clearly spells out the responsibilities—and potential liabilities—of companies and supervisors alike.

The policy of the Gates Corporation and all of its subsidiary companies has always been that all of our employees should be able to enjoy a work atmosphere free from any form of discrimination, including sexual harassment. Even aside from the legal risks, the type of conduct that constitutes sexual harassment is unacceptable and inexcusable in any environment involving the interrelationship of human beings.

Attached is a policy clarifying the Company's position on this issue. Please take the time to read it carefully. This is not a document intended to satisfy the law and be put aside and forgotten; it is a statement of firm policy that will be enforced. Should you have any questions about it, please feel free to contact the Corporate Equal Employment office at extension 2222.

E. J. Busch, Jr.
Director
Corporate Personnel

TO DEPARTMENT HEADS REGARDING
SEXUAL HARASSMENT WORKSHOP

      TO: Staff Department Directors
   FROM: P. J. Ptacek
   SUBJ: SEXUAL HARASSMENT WORKSHOP

Recent guidelines issued by the EEOC have made sexual harassment a violation of Title VII.

To help managers understand this complex area, the Office of Corporate Compliance will present a one-hour informational program at 1:00 P.M. on Thursday, May 12, in the auditorium.

The topics we will discuss are listed below:

- Distinguishing between normal social interaction and behavior that involves a condition of employment for either men or women.
- Investigating allegations of sexual harassment.
- Appropriate disciplinary steps if harassment is discovered.
- Maintaining a work environment free from offensive conduct.

A copy of the new chairman of the board's Bulletin on Sexual Harassment is attached. It will be released next month; the meeting will help you implement the policy.

As you know, all settlement costs associated with EEO charges are billed back to your operating budget, so the meeting will provide a means to minimize your liability.

TO MANAGERS REGARDING WORKSHOP ON
AWARENESS OF SEXUAL HARASSMENT

      TO: All Managers and Supervisors
   FROM: Myrna Mourning
            Affirmative Action Officer
   SUBJ: SEXUAL HARASSMENT AWARENESS WORKSHOP

It has been stated that sexual harassment is one of the major corporate problems of the '80s. Although no figures are available showing the high cost of sexual harassment charges to private business, government statistics indicate that agencies of the federal government paid some $180 million over a two-year period.

In keeping with the Company's policy of treating current issues openly and responsibly, Employee Relations will conduct—for all managers and supervisors—a Sexual Harassment Awareness Workshop. The three major objectives of the workshop are:

1. To provide managers and supervisors avenues to follow in preventing and, if necessary, resolving harassing situations.
2. To assist managers and supervisors in identifying types of behavior that constitutes sexual harassment.
3. To increase managers' and supervisors' understanding of the Equal Employment Opportunity Commission (EEOC) guidelines pertaining to sexual harassment.

The workshop will be held January 10th and 11th in the training room. The Executive Committee has reviewed the program and strongly encourages your attendance because awareness of this issue is important to you and to the company.

Please call Jane Brown in the Employee Relations Department to register for one of the following sessions:

January 10—8:30–11:30 A.M.
January 11—1:00– 3:30 P.M.

TO U.S. DEPARTMENT OF LABOR, OFFICE OF FEDERAL CONTRACT COMPLIANCE PROGRAMS CONCERNING REQUEST FOR DELAY OF DESK AUDIT

Mr. Harold Myers
Acting Denver Area Office Director
U.S. Department of Labor
Office of Federal Contract
   Compliance Programs
2500 Curtis Street, Suite 100
Denver, Colorado 80205

Re: Your Letter NEDN-093, 5/4/——

Dear Mr. Myers:

We received your letter on May 5, 19—— concerning the compliance audit that OFCCP will conduct on Rocky Mountain Oil Company.

Effective May 6, 19——, our Affirmative Action Coordinator started her vacation. This, coupled with a reduction in our clerical staff, results in our request for a two-week extension to the 30-day deadline for the submittal of desk audit information to your office. The additional two weeks will enable us to provide you with complete and accurate data in all categories you requested.

Please advise us of your decision at your earliest convenience.

Sincerely,

John L. Meyer
Director
Human Resources

INFORMING EMPLOYEES ABOUT
EQUAL EMPLOYMENT OPPORTUNITY POLICY:
SAMPLE ONE

TO: All Employees

SUBJ: EQUAL EMPLOYMENT OPPORTUNITY POLICY*

Under its Equal Employment Opportunity policy and its Affirmative Action Program, Sherman & Howard will not discriminate against any employee or applicant for employment because of race, color, religion, sex, national origin, age, or handicap and Sherman & Howard will take affirmative action to insure that applicants are employed and that employees are treated during employment without regard to their race, color, religion, sex, national origin, or handicap.

Sherman & Howard believes that employees should be provided with a working environment free from harassment based on race, color, religion, sex, national origin, or handicap. Racial or ethnic remarks or slurs will not be tolerated. The firm intends to protect its employees, both legal and non-legal staff, from such harassment.

In addition, physical, written, or spoken conduct of a sexual nature by someone in the firm in a position to influence employment decisions constitutes sexual harassment when: (1) submission to such conduct is made either expressly or implicitly a term or condition of an individual's continued employment; or (2) submission to or rejection of such conduct by an individual is used as the basis for employment decisions affecting such individual.

Sexual harassment also includes repeated and unwelcome physical, written, or spoken conduct by either a supervisor or any fellow employee that substantially interferes with an individual's work performance or creates what a reasonable person would consider to be an intimidating, hostile, or offensive working environment.

If an employee believes he or she is being subjected to any of these forms of harassment or believes he or she is being discriminated against because other individuals are receiving favored treatment in exchange for sexual favors, he or she must bring this to the attention of the firm. The very nature of harassment makes it impossible to detect unless the person being harassed registers his or her discontent with the appropriate firm representatives. Consequently, if the firm is to have this information, employees must report offensive conduct. For this purpose employees are instructed to report such situations to the Equal Employment Opportunity Officer.

Complaints and situations reported by employees to these officers will be investigated by them to the extent appropriate in light of the circumstances of the allegations. In cases in which the employee requests that his or her identity not be

*This policy is formulated and used by the law firm of Sherman & Howard. It reflects the status of the law as of May, 1983. Because the law is in a constant state of change, Sherman & Howard makes no representation that this policy will continue to be up to date.

disclosed to the person about whom a complaint or report has been made, the request for anonymity will be honored, if possible. If, after investigation, the firm finds that disciplinary action or termination is justified, such action may be imposed.

I acknowledge that I have read and understand the above anti-harassment policy.

_____   _____
Date   Signature

INFORMING EMPLOYEES ABOUT EQUAL EMPLOYMENT OPPORTUNITY POLICY: SAMPLE TWO

TO: All Employees of
          Western Energy Company

FROM: Wilson F. Jones, President

SUBJ: EQUAL EMPLOYMENT OPPORTUNITY AND
           AFFIRMATIVE ACTION STATEMENT

Western Energy Company subscribes to the concept of Equal Employment Opportunity and Affirmative Action. We judge individuals on job-related factors, without regard to race, color, religion, sex, age, or national origin. We believe this is the most positive way to attract and retain good employees. Fulfilling this belief in nondiscrimination is a real and vital part of everyone's job—a commitment shared by all of us at Western Energy Company.

Since the company's inception, we have subscribed to the letter and the spirit of Equal Employment Opportunity and Affirmative Action. It's more than just a matter of legal compliance; it's our philosophy.

It's also our objective to make sure that all employees have an equal opportunity to progress within the Company. Our Affirmative Action Programs are an important tool in meeting this objective. As part of our continuing efforts to upgrade our employment practices for minorities, women, disabled, and veterans, we monitor their utilization within the Company and periodically reaffirm our commitment to Affirmative Action and Equal Employment Opportunity.

After reviewing the progress we made in our Affirmative Action Programs last year, I'm pleased to report that our efforts have had a positive effect. We still have more to accomplish, however. We will strengthen our efforts to increase our representation of women and minorities at professional and managerial levels.

INFORMING EMPLOYEES ABOUT
EQUAL EMPLOYMENT OPPORTUNITY POLICIES:
SAMPLE THREE

TO: All Employees

FROM: Bob W. Smith
          Director, Human Resources

The Johnson Computer Company has an Affirmative Action Program designed to employ and advance in employment qualified disabled veterans and veterans of the Vietnam era.

If you are a disabled veteran or a veteran of the Vietnam era, please tell us. Submission of this information is voluntary, and refusal to provide it will not subject you to discharge or disciplinary treatment.

A disabled veteran is defined as a person who:

- is entitled to disability compensation under laws administered by the Veterans Administration for disability rated at 30% or more, or a person whose discharge or release from active duty was for a disability incurred or aggravated in the line of duty.
- is capable of performing a particular job with reasonable accommodation to the disability.

A veteran of the Vietnam era is defined as a person who:

- served on active duty for a period of more than 180 days, any part of which occurred between August 5, 1964 and May 7, 1975, and was discharged or released therefrom with other than a dishonorable discharge, or
- was discharged or released from active duty for a service-connected disability, if any part of such active duty was performed between August 5, 1964 and May 7, 1975.

TO MANAGERS PROVIDING
AFFIRMATIVE ACTION UPDATE

TO: Managers and Supervisors

FROM: James L. Lawson
          President

SUBJ: AFFIRMATIVE ACTION UPDATE

Coastal Oil Company continues to enjoy rapid growth in pursuit of business goals. Our outstanding performance as a company is due in large measure to creating and maintaining an organization that achieves a high level of professional excellence through recruitment, development and training, motivation, and fostering a stimulating work environment for all employees.

The selection, promotion, and performance appraisal of individuals based on job-related factors, without regard to race, color, religion, sex, age, national origin, or mental or physical handicap, is an integral part of our human resource program.

Management is committed to ensuring that employment is provided on an equal opportunity basis. Affirmative Action Programs have been implemented and will serve as a guide to assist all of us in moving toward our goals.

Briefing sessions to review our current Affirmative Action Program posture relative to the standards by which we judge ourselves and the goals adopted by management will be held June 14, 15, and 16 in the Sixth Floor Conference Room.

Please arrange your schedule so that you may attend one of these briefing sessions and advise Sharon Hawkins (ext. 425) of the session you will attend.

> Wednesday, June 14—9:00–10:00 A.M.
> Thursday, June 15—9:00–10:00 A.M.
> Friday, June 16—9:00–10:00 A.M.

TO MANAGERS REGARDING AFFIRMATIVE ACTION WORKSHOP

> TO: All Managers and Supervisors
> FROM: Employee Relations
> SUBJ: AFFIRMATIVE ACTION WORKSHOP

An Affirmative Action Workshop will be presented by the Employee Relations staff on July 30 and 31 and August 1st. The workshops will be conducted at the Ramada Inn, I-70 at Kipling, starting at 8:30 A.M. and adjourning at 11:00 A.M. Please arrrange your schedule so that you can attend one of these sessions.

This year's program, in addition to apprising you of any Affirmative Action progress, will include the use of training tools designed to make you more knowledgeable concerning our Affirmative Action Program and Equal Opportunity guidelines. The theme of this year's program, "EEO Is Your Job," is consistent with our philosophy of placing the maximum amount of accountability and decision making in the hands of managers. This philosophy has helped us achieve our objective during the past two years.

Call the Employee Relations department, extension 2902, to indicate which session you will be attending.

9

Letters Regarding Employee Health and Safety

The Personnel Department is certainly not the department of health and hospitals, but it does have a responsibility to employees for maintaining a healthy environment. The tone of this type of correspondence is like most other employee correspondence—short, to the point, but caring and open. You are not a safety or health policeman, but a resource for improvements that may be needed.

At times employees feel threatened or fearful of safety and health issues, so your letters should be non-threatening and informative.

MANAGER'S TIPS ON SAFETY AND HEALTH CORRESPONDENCE

- There is a privacy issue connected with correspondence in this area. Employees want assurance that their privacy will be protected.

- Letters to employees for safety violations should be factual, the tone matter-of-fact, citing regulations and violations, but not chiding or accusing.

**TO WORKER'S COMPENSATION DIVISION
QUESTIONING CLAIM**

The Honorable Joan Lore
Clerk of the District Court
Worker's Compensation Division
P.O. Box 189
Douglas, Wyoming 82633

      Re: M. N. Browne Employee-Claimant vs. Rocky Mountain Energy Company,
           Employer-Respondent; Worker's Compensation Case No. 00012; Converse
           County, Wyoming

Dear Mrs. Lore:

We have been in consultation with Mr. l. M. Dorn, safety supervisor, Rocky
Mountain Energy Company, with respect to claims for medication that have been
filed in referenced case.

After reviewing all claims filed to date, we have concluded that Mr. Browne appears
to be using unusually large amounts of various medications prescribed at too
frequent intervals. None of the claims state the purpose for which the medication
was prescribed and the prescriptions do not appear to have been ordered by a
physician on each occasion.

Neither Mr. Browne, his doctors, nor the medical pharmacy personnel have
properly filed their claims under the applicable Worker's Compensation regulation.
On numerous occasions all of the claimants have been instructed by the Clerk of
Court that they must properly file their claims in order to receive payment and
were advised that the prescriptions were not supported with proper medical
authorization.

Based upon the forgoing, we have advised Mr. Dorn to deny any and all further
claims filed in this matter until such time as the present claims are properly
presented.

Attached hereto for the Court's review as Exhibit A is a summary of the drugs in
question.

Sincerely,

Mary H. Henderson
Legal Assistant
Natural Resources

TO VICE-PRESIDENT PROVIDING INFORMATION
ON THE COMPANY SAFETY RECORD

Mr. Laurence A. Haley
Vice-President
Human Resources
H. C. Wilson Corporation
1062 Highway 70
Pittsburgh, Pennsylvania 15216

Dear Laurence:

The Pittsburgh Regulator Division of the H. C. Wilson Corporation recorded a
total of injuries resulting in 45 lost work days during the first quarter of 19——.

Eight of the 11 departments completed the quarter without a lost workday. The
Process Department worked 150 consecutive days without a lost workday injury or
accident. This excellent record was broken, however, on February 10, when a
mechanic sustained a back injury while lifting a 100-pound steel plate.

There were 37 accidents during the quarter; ten involved property damage, for a
total of $4,340, and 27 resulted in personal injury.

Overall, we feel this is a good track record. It is a marked improvement over the
last quarter, and we will continue our efforts to improve the Regulator Division's
safety record.

Sincerely,

Victor P. Timmons
Manager
Safety and Health

TO EMPLOYEES REGARDING
SAFETY RECOGNITION PROGRAM

TO:	All Employees
FROM:	Hugh Williams
	Safety Manager
SUBJ:	SAFETY RECOGNITION AND AWARDS PROGRAM

The Safety Recognition and Awards Program is designed to recognize outstanding
individual and work-group safety performance when established safety
performance benchmarks are achieved. The benchmarks are achievable if the

program is effectively communicated and properly used as a means of stimulating and maintaining employee interest and cooperation in your operation's formal Safety and Health Plan.

It is company policy to provide safe and healthful working conditions and employ safe work practices at all company operations. The goal is to maintain a high level of safety performance companywide. The level of success achieved is directly related to the degree of participation and support given to the Safety and Health Plan by each and every employee in the company within the scope of his or her job.

This program will be modified and updated as necessary to maintain effectiveness and interest.

The enclosed policy should be added to your Safety Manual.

TO MANAGER REGARDING ACCIDENT REPORT FORMS

Mr. Lincoln D. Strong
Manager, Health and Safety
Gibbons Construction Company
P.O. Box 2009
Denver, Colorado 80215

Dear Linc:

In a recent meeting when I met with a group of our people in Grand Junction, they indicated that they have no accident report forms. In addition to not having the forms on hand, they say that many of the people do not understand the difference between the Workman's Compensation form and the Company Accident Report form. They feel they need a written procedure to follow.

They also mentioned that their having to send the accident reports to you from Grand Junction and wait for them to be returned has caused problems for them in trying to meet the ten-day deadline for filing the reports. They would prefer to file them directly and send you a photocopy, if that would be agreeable. John Black would be a good person to handle the reports for the Grand Junction office.

I thought I'd pass this information on so you can give them some assistance as soon as possible.

Sincerely,

Gary L. Bowen
Personnel Manager

TO EMPLOYEES REGARDING
MEDICAL EMERGENCY CARDS

TO: All Denver Clinic Employees
FROM: Carolyn L. Hayes, R.N., B.S.
Administrator
Occupational, Environmental, and Preventive Medicine
SUBJ: ATTACHED MEDICAL EMERGENCY CARDS

Please complete the attached medical emergency card and return it to Personnel. It is in your best interest to fill it out in its entirety so that expedient care can be rendered in your behalf as quickly as possible.

For those female employees who may become pregnant sometime in the future, the name of your attending physician and hospital choice for delivery should be made known to Personnel as the due date draws near. A contact person is also suggested so that a phone call can be made.

TO EMPLOYEES REGARDING USE OF FITNESS CENTER

TO: All RME Employees
FROM: Carolyn L. Hayes, R.N.
SUBJ: USE OF FITNESS CENTER

A. Use of the Fitness Center

All those who have been engaged in physical exercise on a regular basis may continue their current exercise routine and are welcome to use the Fitness Center. You can schedule a fitness evaluation after the group described below has been evaluated.

In the interest of medical and physical safety, those employees who have not been engaging in regular exercise, those who have any type of medical problem, and those who may presently be at high risk (i.e., on medications or with elevated blood pressure, elevated body weight, or known high cholesterol) are asked to have a fitness evaluation before beginning to use the Fitness Center. You can schedule your evaluation by calling me at extension 3180.

B. Fitness Evaluation

The fitness evaluation will include any or all of the following components depending on age (34 and under, over 35), medical history, and habits.

Components:

1. Baseline vital signs: temperature, pulse, respirations, and blood pressure.
2. Medical questionnaire and interview to go over history.
3. Height and weight.

4. Lab work consisting of a urine sample and a blood sample for baseline levels (HDL, hematocrit, glucose, BUN, sodium, potassium, uric acid, cholesterol, and triglycerides). If you have had this blood work done within the past year, you are requested to secure a copy of the results so that this test is not repeated.

Those who show one or more risk factors may be requested to undergo additional testing, such as a stress treadmill and/or a basic physical exam by the company-designated physician.

C. Use of Equipment

During the initial phase of use, it is possible that the capacity of the Fitness Center will be exceeded during any time period. In that event it will be necessary for you to reschedule your exercise time.

For those not familiar with the equipment, demonstrations* will be given hourly on Tuesday, January 20, by Jim Woods of Pro-Health Systems. You are requested not to use any piece of equipment if you are not familiar with it. Safe and effective use depends upon your understanding of the equipment.

D. Fitness Center Schedule

As a result of the Fitness Center questionnaire, the following schedule will be used initially to meet the needs of the 160 respondents.

7:00 A.M. to 8:00 A.M.	Coed
8:00 A.M. to 11:00 A.M.	Men
11:00 A.M. to 2:00 P.M.	Coed
2:00 P.M. to 5:00 P.M.	Women
5:00 P.M. to 6:00 P.M.	Coed

This schedule applies Monday through Friday. The Fitness Center will open at 7:00 A.M. and close at 6:00 P.M. As the Center evolves, changes in the current schedule may be necessary to accommodate the needs of the majority of the participants. Also, special informal and formal education programs will be scheduled during the year.

---

*Demonstrations will be from 10:00 A.M. until 4:00 P.M. on Tuesday, January 20.

TO EMPLOYEES AND SPOUSES
REGARDING BLOOD DONOR PROGRAM

TO: All Employees and Spouses

FROM: Carolyn L. Hayes, R.N., B.S.
Administrator
Occupational, Environmental, and Preventive Medicine

SUBJ: BLOOD DONOR PROGRAM FOR THE COMMUNITY OF COLORADO

A blood donor supplies the food for people who go through windshields and red lights. For somebody with leukemia. For people being operated on. For barefoot kids who aren't careful. For people feudin' and fightin'. For hemophiliacs so they can be as normal as possible. For daredevils. For people undergoing dialysis while waiting for a kidney transplant. For people who fool around with guns. For little kids who manage to uncap a bottle full of something poisonous. For people who are burned pretty badly. For new mothers needing a transfusion. For new babies who need a complete change of blood supply. For people having open heart surgery. For cancer patients. For people with a severe case of hepatitis. For kids who fall out of trees or whatever. For anybody any age with bleeding ulcers. For people in the wrong place at the wrong time. For the very tired with severe anemia. For people who run into things. For people who are in a lot worse shape than most people you know. —<u>American Red Cross</u>.

Do you know someone who fits into one of these categories? Have you ever wondered if there was anything you could do for them? Did you know there is something you can do? Be a buddy to your buddy or your buddy's buddy and give a pint of blood when Belle Bonfils comes on March 17, 19———.

The cost of giving blood is minimal. It takes less than an hour for a donor to go through the channels of giving blood. As a blood donor you not only receive the satisfaction of knowing you've done someone a lot of good in the Denver community, perhaps saved a life, but you receive a "mini-physical." During this "mini-physical" your blood pressure, pulse, hemoglobin level, and blood will be checked. This free screening could detect health care problems that can be prevented due to early detection.

The only way to get blood is through the veins of a human being. At this time, no machine or computer can produce blood. It is up to the individual to share one of a dozen pints circulating through his or her body. By donating one pint of your own blood every eight weeks, others can be helped and protected by insuring a constant and adequate supply to the people of Colorado.

Be a buddy and take a buddy to give blood on March 17, when Belle Bonfils visits. Employees are encouraged to bring their spouses in this response to a vital community need. Donors will be scheduled every 15 minutes, four at a time, between 9 A.M. and 3 P.M. Appointments can be made by calling Carolyn Hayes at extension 258. A reminder card will be sent back to each donor as appointments are made.

Consider this: If fewer people were to give blood, less would be available to use for urgent surgery patients or emergency accident victims, not to mention all the others who require allotments of blood in order to live. If no one had the time to administer blood or were too scared to start a blood transfusion, many people would lose the gift of life.

Remember, you'll be giving the gift of life, so lie down and be counted as a blood donor. Blood is only good for 32 days; I hope someone would have given if you or your family ever needed blood.

My thanks.

REGARDING AUTHORIZATION OF CHILD'S MEDICAL TREATMENT

TO: All Employees

FROM: Carolyn L. Hayes, R.N., B.S.
       Administrator
       Occupational, Environmental,
       and Preventive Medicine

SUBJ: AUTHORIZATION FOR YOUR CHILD'S MEDICAL TREATMENT

Attached is a form provided for you in the event you are away from your child and have entrusted the care of your child to another. The document does not have to be notarized nor does it have to be witnessed. The release should be kept in a safe but accessible place in the event your child needs medical attention. If you would like another form for a friend or relative, please let me know.

Please secure the medical information on your child so that appropriate and complete medical care may be administered in your absence.

TO MANAGERS REGARDING EMPLOYEE ASSISTANCE PROGRAM

To Managers of Salaried Personnel:

The attached article, highlighting the Gates Employee Assistance Program, should remind us of the excellent help we have available, as managers and supervisors, whenever we see our employees having a performance problem for which there seems to be no readily discernible cause.

Because our employee assistance program maintains a low profile, it is easy to forget that the program was started by Gates to help with performance problems of production workers and salaried employees alike. The success of the plan has led many employees, on their own, to seek help from the Gates counselors for marital, emotional, drug, or alcohol problems. But the program continues to provide the opportunity to help all of our employees work their way through personal problems that may be affecting job performance.

Roman "Tony" Valdez and Tony Sanchez are both available for consultation, whenever you believe you may have a performance problem of this kind in your area. Just call extension 1111 for a discussion with either of them.

E. J. Busch, Jr.
Director
Corporate Personnel

TO EMPLOYEES ADVISING THEM OF COMPANY POLICY ON EMPLOYEE PROBLEMS AFFECTING PERFORMANCE

TO: The Family of Burgess Corporation Employees

The purpose of this letter is to personally acquaint you with our new policy on employee problems affecting job performance and attendance. The new program, beginning operation September 1, 19——, is called the Employee Assistance Program (EAP). It is available to all salaried and hourly employees and their immediate families, as defined by existing insurance coverage. The program deals with a wide range of human situations that, if unattended, can result in unsatisfactory job performance and attendance. Since such problems generally affect the entire family, we are notifying employees and their families separately.

At Burgess, we are aware that human troubles not directly associated with one's job function can have an adverse effect on job performance and attendance. In some instances, neither the efforts of the employee nor the supervisor are successful in resolving the employee's difficulty, and unsatisfactory job performance persists.

We believe that almost any human problem can be successfully dealt with if it is properly identified and constructive motivation for correction is provided. This applies whether we are talking about inappropriate consumption of alcohol or other drugs, family or marital distress, financial trouble, nervous or emotional disorders, or other concerns. While the company is primarily concerned with job performance, experience shows that the cause of the problems must be dealt with first. The company also realizes that proper diagnosis of such causes is best done by someone who is professionally trained and competent.

We want you to know that assistance is available on a confidential and professional basis without jeopardizing your future or your reputation. You need only contact me to get further information.

Our purpose in establishing this program is to help people with difficulties get the assistance they need at the earliest possible time. The alternative is that such difficulties, if unattended, get worse, and employees can jeopardize their jobs.

We hope the new EAP will be of service to you if such problems exist for you or someone in your immediate family.

Sincerely,

Edwin L. Burgess
President

TO DOCTOR APOLOGIZING FOR EMPLOYEES WHO HAVE BEEN TARDY TO APPOINTMENTS

David R. Hunter, M.D.
Internal Medicine Group
255 South Madison Street
Denver, Colorado 80209

Dear Dr. Hunter:

Please accept our apologies for the inconvenience several of our employees caused by canceling their appointments at the last minute. We have taken steps to remedy the situation by explaining to them the problems that arise when they miss an appointment without calling and canceling in advance.

I'd like to take this opportunity to let you know what a fine job we feel you are doing for our group. Many of our people have come by to say that it's the best, most comprehensive physical they've ever had.

Please let me know if anything develops in the future that concerns our company, and thank you again for your help.

Sincerely yours,

Eugene M. Schoulte
Personnel Manager

TO EMPLOYEES REGARDING BUILDING SECURITY

        TO: All Employees
    FROM: Luther L. Thompson
    SUBJ: BUILDING SECURITY

Most of you are aware of the serious incident that occurred in our building lobby on Wednesday, April 13, 19——. A disoriented man—a discharged employee of a firm that performs security services for us—entered the building carrying a loaded, double-barreled shotgun. Several employees diverted his attention until the police arrived, at which time he was disarmed and removed.

Although the police and courts are taking the matter seriously and a relatively high bond has been set, it is likely that the man will secure release from custody in the near future.

Because of the prospective presence of this individual in our community, we are concerned about the safety of the people employed in our building. We plan to take additional security precautions and seek your cooperation as follows:

1. Starting Monday, April 18, the north lobby doors will be open between 7:30 and 8:00 A.M. only. An employee or a security guard will monitor the people entering the building during this period. If an individual is not recognized, he or she will not be permitted to enter until further verification is obtained.

2. All entrances to the building will remain locked, except as noted above. The north lobby and the second floor east galleria doors are equipped with card readers. Employees can enter through these doors at all times by using their security entry cards. If you have misplaced your entry card and need a new one, contact Employee Relations.
   For fire safety reasons, you will be able to exit from any door, as is presently the case.

3. The south lobby doors will also remain locked, and visitors will be required to enter through the north lobby doors. Visitors will be asked to state their names and the person they are visiting. Only after the receptionist verifies this information with the employee expecting the visitors will they be allowed to enter the lobby area.
Building employees expecting visitors should alert the receptionist in advance to facilitate their guests' entrance.

4. Other protective measures will be taken, including retention of an outside safety patrol service.

In order for the increased security measures to be effective, they require the cooperation of everyone in the building. The doors will remain locked and should not be propped open. Any unusual situations or observations, either in the building or on the grounds, should be reported immediately to the receptionist (ext. 3311).

I realize these precautions may cause some personal inconvenience. However, I believe the actions are necessary to ensure the safety of all of our employees.

10

Letters Regarding Labor Relations, Layoffs, Terminations, and Union Matters

Many indicators point to the 1980's as the decade of employee rights. Letters in these areas must be complete and factual. The recent number of wrongful discharge suits is alarming. Wrongful discharge relates to implied contract theories. An employer's written or oral communication can imply a contractual agreement such as a promise of continued employment or certain benefits.

Wrongful discharge suits have proliferated as the courts have become more responsive to the idea. Wrongful discharge is now expressly recognized in at least 14 states. These include California, Connecticut, Illinois, Indiana, Maryland, Massachusetts, Michigan, New Hampshire, New Jersey, Ohio, Oregon, Pennsylvania, Washington, and West Virginia. Courts in 10 or 12 other states have said they'd recognize the doctrine in appropriate cases.

MANAGER'S TIPS ON LABOR RELATIONS

- Supervisors and managers should be instructed not to write anything about job rights or benefits that may be inconsistent with company policy. They should be especially careful to avoid giving employees broad assurances in writing about job rights, benefits, or terminations. If you get into a wrongful discharge situation, rely on legal counsel.
- Letters regarding union relations should avoid conflict. State the facts and review the issues.

Interestingly enough, the Association of Governing Boards reports that 46 percent of National Labor Relations Board-sponsored elections in the past few years have resulted in rejections of unions by white- and blue-collar workers alike. A significant portion of the rejection stems from dissatisfaction with the inevitability of conflict between labor and management.

Letters regarding layoff or termination should be concise, state the reasons for termination, all the facts surrounding the termination, and the benefits the employee will receive.

The tone of labor relations letters is business-like with the content factual and concise; the human relations side is honest but not legalistic or verbose.

TO REPRESENTATIVE OF WAGE-HOUR DIVISION
OF THE DEPARTMENT OF LABOR REGARDING CLAIM

Mr. Jonathan Wright
Wage-Hour Division
Department of Labor
1800 Sherman Street
Denver, Colorado 80203

Dear Mr. Wright:

In response to your request for information on our hours of work, we provide the following work schedules:

Day Shift
8:00 A.M. to 5:00 P.M.
One hour paid for lunch

Night Shift
5:00 P.M. to 2:00 A.M.
One hour paid for dinner

We have investigated the claim by Mrs. Jennie Welsh. She feels that she should be paid for overtime because she reported to work 15 minutes early every day and took only one half-hour for lunch for a period of three months, commencing July 5, 19—— and ending October 7, 19——.

Our investigation shows that Mrs. Welsh did in fact work these hours. They were not her regularly scheduled hours, however, and she completed her time cards as having worked 8:00 A.M. to 5:00 P.M. each day with a one-hour lunch period.

Mrs. Welsh's supervisor substantiates her claim. It is not company policy to allow employees to change their work schedules. However, because her supervisor allowed the altered schedule, we feel an obligation to reimburse Mrs. Welsh for the overtime of three hours and forty-five minutes per week for the three-month period.

We have instituted an audit of our procedures and payroll records to ensure that other employees have not participated in similar practices. If you need further information or explanation of the claim, please give me a call.

Sincerely,

Walter M. Thompson
Personnel Manager
Staley Manufacturing Company

REGARDING FEASIBILITY STUDY
OF NEW PROJECT
BASED ON LABOR RELATIONS CLIMATE

Mr. John H. Bell
Cortez Mining Company
717 Seventeenth Street
Denver, Colorado 80202

Dear John:

We are moving ahead to update the feasibility study of the Buffalo Project. Planning is underway and cost estimates are being developed, which are due the end of June.

We have been asked to provide benefit levels, labor wage rates, and a review of the labor relations climate. I would appreciate your investigating local company practices and providing this information to me by June 10th.

Please give me a call if you have any questions.

Sincerely,

Brad Andrews
Personnel Director

REGARDING LABOR RELATIONS ANALYSIS

    TO: R. W. Parsons
FROM: Mary Cook
           Personnel Manager
  SUBJ: BLUE MOUNTAIN PROJECT

Pursuant to our conversation, we will commence gathering preliminary data on the following items in support of the Blue Mountain project:

1. Labor cost analysis, including rates and benefits.
2. Review of pertinent area labor agreements.
3. Labor force analyses in the area.
4. Review manning table data as available for surface mines—truck/shovel dragline operation, for two 7–8 million TPY operations.
5. Labor relations environment.

As your project progresses and dates become more firm as to when you will need this data, let us know.

In the meantime, we'll begin our preliminary work. As the project progresses and other items come to mind where we might assist you, please give us a call.

REGARDING LABOR RELATIONS OVERVIEW

TO: L. T. Hunt
FROM: F. B. Cox
Industrial Relations Manager
SUBJ: LABOR RELATIONS OVERVIEW—TRINIDAD, COLORADO

BACKGROUND

Trinidad is located in Las Animas County along the Purgatorie River in southwestern Colorado. Historically, Trinidad was an important settlement along the Santa Fe Trail and a crossroads for the stagecoach and railroad lines. Because of the availability of coal supplies and the demand for coal by the railroads, numerous "coal mining camps" developed in the country. With Trinidad as the economic center of the activity, a virtual boom period was experienced until the 1930's, when coal mining began to decline. Recently, because of the current search for reliable energy sources, a new emphasis is being placed on coal in Las Animas County. Colorado Fuel and Iron has opened a new shaft, and other coal companies are currently investigating opportunities in the area.

POPULATION

The 19—— Trinidad population was estimated at 11,000. It declined approximately 7 percent between the 19—— and 19—— census periods. Due primarily to community development efforts, the population has now ceased its decline and begun an upward trend.

Approximately 48 percent of the population is Spanish-American, 50 percent is Anglo, and 2 percent Black, Indian, and other groups. The Anglo group is primarily of Italian descent. Almost 48 percent of Las Animas County families have income in excess of $10,000 per year; over 29 percent have annual incomes greater than $15,000.

LABOR AND WAGES

According to 19—— statistics, there were 5,700 in the work force. The five largest commercial or service employers are as follows:

CF&I's Allen & Maxwell Mines	650 UMWA
Colorado & Southern Railroad	330—various unions
School District #1	200
City of Trinidad and	325 full time
Trinidad Junior College	135 part time

The community also has three seasonal industries: farm products, livestock, and tourism. The labor force of Trinidad is drawn from a forty-mile radius that includes Walsenburg, Colorado; Raton, New Mexico; and several small surrounding rural communities.

The major unions in the area are:

United Mine Workers of America
Construction Worker's Union
Maintenance & Public Service Local 354
Carpenter's Union

The United Mine Workers has a long history in the Trinidad area and continues to be the prominent union.

PERFORMANCE APPRAISAL
AFTER THREE-MONTH PROBATIONARY PERIOD

TO: John Doe Personnel File
FROM: J. A. Compton
SUBJ: PERFORMANCE APPRAISAL

The three-month probationary program for John Doe has now been completed. The program, which provided specific assignments to be finalized and reviewed by the Marketing Department, was designed to measure progress in correcting the following major deficiencies (see previous memo dated November 22, 19——):

- Written analyses not completed on time and of unacceptable quality.
- Minimal interaction with counterparts and managers in Marketing, Law, and Diversification, and other areas crucial to Mr. Doe's success.

Based on review of the assignments by other appropriate people as well as myself, and based on observations of attitude and interest level, it has been concluded that John Doe has *not* fully met the requirements of the probationary program. This conclusion considers the following:

- The Laurel Canyon marketability assessment was determined not to have <u>fully met</u> requirements and suggestions for revision were not incorporated into the final draft.
- The Colorado Canyon acquisition analysis was not undertaken in a timely fashion, resulting in a delay of the entire project.
- The Brown County presentation to the Management Committee <u>did not meet</u> requirements. The presentation came across poorly; it appeared as if Mr. Doe was not prepared and did not understand his subject matter; and no substantive information was distributed as planned.
- Continuing development and managing of the Market Research data base system <u>did not meet</u> requirements. Critical discussions between John and others in the Marketing Department, to determine what was needed in the system and on how to make it most useful, did not occur. Reports of meetings were written only after repeated reminders from me.

The above discussion documents the lack of adequate progress in correcting deficiencies. The decision has been made, therefore, to terminate John Doe's employment effective March 7, 19——.

REGARDING EMPLOYEE'S PERFORMANCE STATUS

TO: L. W. Winthrop
FROM: R. A. Meade
SUBJ: PERFORMANCE STATUS

This memo is intended to confirm our discussion that your performance has become unacceptable. After our discussion in October 19—— you made substantial improvement. Due to this improvement during the fourth quarter of 19——, you were rated as "fully adequate" in January 19——. It was hoped the emphasis of that performance would be a positive encouragement to your continued improvement. However, your performance over the last several months has again slipped into "unacceptable."

1. Your ability to analyze a business situation and design the appropriate system continues to be a problem. You still have difficulty in seeing the goal of the system and maintaining enough flexibility to implement a system to meet the goal that has been identified. In many cases, the systems that you designed have required significant review by a systems analyst to be functional. Quarterly estimates and the tape review for the Olsen conversion were two examples we discussed during our meeting. In each case, significant revisions were identified during the review process.

   Some responsibility for the tracking of project requests does reside with the systems analyst. However, as a programmer/analyst, it is your responsibility to perform detail design work, and to track your own projects through to completion. In the past, assistance with detail definition at the beginning of the project has been required, as well as a detail level checking by a systems analyst, to ensure that your project has been completed as scheduled.

   A programmer/analyst should not require the level of pre-definition or detail review you have been needing over the last four months. To successfully perform at a programmer/analyst level, you must perform basic detail design work and be prepared to meet your project dates in a timely fashion, without a detailed review by project leaders.

2. Your ability to function as a viable member of a project team is still not at an acceptable level. You seem to function best when detail specifications are provided to you and you can work on the specifications, regardless of other activities around you, and then provide results for detailed review. The team concept is critical to successful system development. This requires that each member of the team not only work on his or her assigned area, but also contribute to the team with suggestions and support as needed.

3. Although some improvement was shown following your position adjustment last October to programmer/analyst, your overall cooperation and attitude are again unacceptable. You continue to exhibit an "adversary" relationship with management personnel and project leaders with whom you work. The ability to communicate effectively is imperative in your continued role as a programmer/analyst.

4. Because of the problems mentioned above, work tasks assigned to you have been substandard for the programmer/analyst position. In many cases, the tasks that have been assigned would have been performed by a programmer or junior programmer. It is important for you to realize that we cannot afford to classify you as a programmer/analyst and not assign full programmer/analyst responsibilities to you with confidence that the appropriate communication, analysis, and team effort will be provided.

Over the next three months (until August 1, 19——), I will track your performance very closely and provide monthly written performance appraisals. In the past, you have had a tendency to make short-term improvements and then have "old problems" return again. Clearly, it is now up to you to bring your performance to an acceptable level on a continued basis or you will be subject to termination.

WRITTEN WARNING FOR EXCESSIVE ABSENTEEISM:
SAMPLE ONE

Mr. John Doe
6570 West 23rd Place
Omaha, Nebraska 68131

Dear John:

In accordance with company policy, this memorandum is to serve as a written warning for your excessive absences. You must immediately improve your attendance record to acceptable standards or further discipline, including termination, may result.

On several occasions I have spoken to you about your poor attendance record, and improvement would be noticed for a time. However, your excessive absences always resumed. For the period covering January 1 through August 31, you were absent 62 days, excluding vacations and normal holidays. These absences are detailed below:

Reason	Days
Illness	37
Excused with pay	8½
Excused without pay	16½
Total	62 days

In our discussion on September 11, 19——, you agreed to consult with the company nurse concerning health, or to enroll in the new company Employee Assistance program. I agreed to provide you the necessary time that you may need for consultations and examinations by any company-authorized professionals. You should realize, however, that failure to enroll in the EAP or any unauthorized absences from this date on will be grounds for your immediate dismissal.

Sincerely,

William H. Carter
Director
Personnel Services

WARNING FOR EXCESSIVE ABSENTEEISM:
SAMPLE TWO

TO:	Bill Smiley
FROM:	Louise Browne
	Personnel Manager
SUBJ:	WRITTEN WARNING FOR EXCESSIVE ABSENTEEISM

Bill, you were given a verbal warning Tuesday, February 26, 19—— regarding your excessive absenteeism during the past three months of your employment. Since your date of hire, which was July 2, 19——, until now, you have been absent the following dates:

Monday	1/14/	8 hours	yes, called in
Friday	1/25/	8 hours	no call
Monday	2/04/	8 hours	yes, called in
Friday	2/15/	8 hours	yes, called in
Monday	2/25/	8 hours	yes, called in
Monday	3/03/	8 hours	yes, called in
Friday	3/21/	8 hours	no call
Friday	3/28/	8 hours	no call
Tuesday	4/08/	8 hours	yes, called in
Thursday	5/08/	8 hours	yes, called in

Since no improvement has been made toward reducing your absenteesim, we believe this written warning is necessary.

You were absent 80 hours, for a total of 7.8 percent. This percentage is calculated on a time period from 1/02/—— through 7/02/—— (1040 hours). We would like to see your absenteeism reduced to a level of 5 percent or less.

You have been advised to call in directly to your supervisor within two hours of your start time. Your start time is 7:30 A.M. and, therefore, you must call in by 9:30 A.M. You have also been advised to call in each day you are absent. On three occasions, you failed to notify your supervisor of your intended absence.

Your absenteeism problem must be corrected immediately, and must remain corrected, or your employment may be terminated. If you have problems that need discussion, please do not hesitate to talk them over with me or your supervisor. We will support you in your efforts to remedy this situation.

INFORMING EMPLOYEE OF BEING PLACED ON 30-DAY FORMAL PROBATION

Ms. Linda M. Smith
1732 Simms Street
Lakewood, Colorado 80215

As a result of your unsatisfactory performance during the past six months, and your failure to correct this record after verbal discussions and written warning, you are now being placed on a 30-day formal probation, effective July 9, 19—— through August 8, 19——.

As we discussed earlier, the reason for this probationary period is your chronic absenteeism and continual lack of punctuality. Over the past four months, you have been absent 30 days and late 12 times, ranging between 15 minutes and one hour.

The targets we agreed upon for your period of probation are:

1. You will not be absent during the entire period of probation. Should absolute necessity, however, require absence, you will inform me prior to the absence, or, if an unexpected emergency arises, you will phone immediately in the morning and later give written justification of the absolute necessity for the absence; and

2. You will not be late more than twice during the probation period, and at no time will you be more than five minutes late.

I have scheduled a counseling session on July 20, 19—— to meet with you and evaluate your progress during this period. Additionally, I would like to assure you that I will be available for discussions and counseling at any other time during this probation to provide any assistance you may require. I sincerely hope that this action will result in correction of this problem. Failure to correct this situation, however, will result in termination of your employment, either at the end of the probationary period, or before that time if no positive improvement is evident during the early stages of the probation.

		Supervisor	Date
		Supervisor's Manager	Date
Employee's Acknowledgment	Date	Personnel Manger	Date

LETTER INFORMING EMPLOYEE OF DISCIPLINARY ACTION

Dale L. Bradley
8796 Dawn Drive
Denver, Colorado 80203

Dear Dale:

The purpose of this letter is to describe the events that have occurred over the past several weeks, which have resulted in the need for disciplinary action, and to inform you of the conduct required on your part for continued employment with ROC.

On Thursday, January 19, 19——, you left your work assignment in Washington, D.C., without the permission of your supervisor and traveled to Miami, Florida, for personal reasons. On Friday, January 20, George Long attempted to reach you at your hotel in Washington, D.C., and was told by the desk clerk that you were no longer registered. Unaware that George had tried to reach you, you subsequently called him from Miami and told him you were still on the job in Washington. Your phone call from Miami was placed a few minutes after George had called for you in Washington. On February 1, you submitted your expense report to your supervisor and falsified the dates you were on the job in Washington, D.C. Inconsistencies between your expense report and the hotel receipt were noticed by your supervisor. During a review of this matter, you admitted that (a) you had left Washington, D.C., on January 19; (b) you had called George Long from Miami on January 20 and told him you were on the job in Washington; and (c) you falsified your expense statement to reflect that you were in Washington, D.C., on January 20.

These recent events have resulted in the culmination of a growing concern that I have been experiencing over the past several months relative to increasingly frequent confrontations you have had with both your fellow employees and outside business contacts.

As I have discussed with you, the acts of deception attendant to the above matter, together with the incidents of confrontation, are unacceptable and will not be permitted by either myself or executive management of ROC. Accordingly, I am placing you on disciplinary probation for a period of six months from the date of this letter. During this period, I will carefully monitor your work activities, placing particular emphasis on your interpersonal relationships with your fellow employees and outside individuals.

Any further incidents observed during this period that are contrary to acceptable standards of behavior will result in your immediate dismissal.

Dale, we want you to succeed, and we hope that your acknowledgment of the seriousness of this situation will have a positive result on your future at Rankin Oil Company.

Sincerely,

Stanley Bishop
Personnel Director

TO MANAGERS REGARDING
TERMINATION PROCEDURES

      TO: All Managers
FROM: Bradley Williams
           Personnel Manager
 SUBJ: TERMINATION PROCEDURES

The Payroll Department and the Employee Relations Department encountered significant difficulty during the month of August in receiving notices of termination. Because of these problems, we thought it appropriate at this time to restate the procedures that need to be followed to properly complete a termination.

In the case of a voluntary termination, where advance notice is given, the Employee Profile form should be sent to the personnel coordinator in the Employee Relations Department as soon as notice is received. The termination will be processed and the Payroll Department will prepare a final check.

For an involuntary termination, the Employee Profile form should be completed and furnished to the personnel coordinator in the Employee Relations Department as far in advance as possible, so the final check can be prepared and delivered to you prior to termination. If, for some reason, this is not feasible, let us know. A final check must be provided to a terminated employee within 24 hours of termination.

If the termination is for a non-exempt employee, the final time card indicating the number of hours last worked should also be submitted with the Employee Profile form. If you do not process the termination form in a timely fashion, it could result in an employee's not receiving the final paycheck promptly. There is also the possibility that lack of adequate information contained on the termination form would result in the company's failure to collect an employee cash advance. In the case of an involuntary termination, we need to review the circumstances surrounding the termination before final action is taken. Please check with me or with Larry Hanson or Ron Brown.

It is our policy not to terminate employees unless they have been properly counseled regarding their situation and have been given an opportunity to correct the deficiency or take necessary corrective action. While there may be exceptions in cases of serious offenses, the counseling normally includes at least one written warning notice.

A copy of any written warning should be forwarded to the Employee Relations Department.

Upon notice of a termination, our department conducts an exit interview. The results of exit interviews are available to all managers and vice-presidents above the terminating employee. The exit interview report is retained in the Employee Relations Department.

If you have any questions on terminations, please give me a call.

TO VICE-PRESIDENT
PROVIDING TURNOVER REPORT

Mr. L. G. Stanton
Vice-President, Employee Relations
Rocky Mountain Oil Company
Post Office Box 2001
Denver, Colorado 80202

      Re: Turnover Report

Dear Larry:

The enclosed statistics may be of value to you. I know we have discussed them in the past, but this letter is more reliable than my memory.

Exempt are those salaried persons who are defined as not eligible for overtime payment. Non-exempt are those who are paid for overtime, and hourly is self-explanatory.

The non-exempt group is considerably higher in turnover than other areas for several reasons. Most jobs are unskilled and therefore command lower income than the area average. If you have questions regarding the turnover report please give me a call.

Sincerely,

Jack Banner
Manager of Operations
Encls.

TURNOVER RATE

	HOURLY	NON-EXEMPT	EXEMPT	TOTAL TURNOVER
19——	19.49%	37.25%	14.29%	20.28%
19——	17.95%	35.42%	15.15%	18.99%
19——	19.71%	33.33%	9.35%	18.98%
19——	11.59%	16.36%	8.47%	11.42%
19——	7.64%	17.46%	6.11%	8.27%
January	.42%	1.59%	–	.45%
February	.64%	–	–	.45%
March	1.04%	–	.72%	.73%
April	.42%	1.49%	1.44%	.73%
May	.83%	1.49%	.72%	.87%
June	1.04%	2.99%	.71%	1.16%
July	1.67%	3.08%	.71%	1.61%
August	–	1.49%	–	.15%
September	.84%	1.49%	.70%	.87%
October	.21%	–	–	.15%
November	.42%	3.03%	.68%	.73%
December	.21%	–	–	.15%

TURNOVER INCLUDES ALL SEPARATIONS. The annual turnover rates are calculated by dividing the number of separations in each area by the starting workforce in that area. (Example: 19—— hourly had 36 separations with a starting hourly force of 471; therefore, 36 divided by 471 = 7.64%.)

Total turnover is calculated by dividing the sum of hourly, non-exempt, and exempt separations for the year by the starting total workforce. (Example: 19—— separations: hourly—36, non-exempt—11, exempt—8, total separations—55 divided by total workforce of 665; therefore, 55 divided by 665 = 8.27%.)

The monthly figures for 19—— were calculated by dividing the separations in a given month by the corresponding total in each area. (Example: January, 19—— —2 hourly separations, a starting force of 471; therefore, 2 divided by 471 = .42%.)

TO EMPLOYEE REGARDING
A REDUCTION IN WORKFORCE

Mr. Fred L. Fine
14390 32nd Avenue
Golden, Colorado 80401

Dear Fred:

Because of current economic conditions and our inability to finalize several of our current projects on a timely basis, we have found it necessary to have a reduction in force, and we are terminating your employment effective October 8, 19——. The company agrees to pay you, however, for an additional 30 days through November 7, 19——; all unused 19—— vacation and accrued 19—— vacation; plus severance pay at the rate of two weeks for each year of service up to a maximum of 26 weeks.

You understand and agree that this severance payment is in lieu of all other payments and benefits due you as a result of your employment at Western Energy Company and its affiliate companies except those payments and benefits specifically identified in this letter.

In addition to termination pay, severance pay, and vacation pay, the company will pay your medical insurance coverage through December 19——. All other benefits cease October 8, 19——.

The company is also prepared to provide job search counseling and résumé assistance to those employees who request it. Please notify us that you wish to receive these services no later than October 15, 19——.

A letter reviewing specific details of your particular benefits and severance pay will be mailed to your home October 10, 19——.

Sincerely,

Fred K. Adams
Director Human Resources
Western Energy Company

TO EMPLOYEES REGARDING A REDUCTION IN FORCE

TO:	All Salt Lake City Employees
FROM:	Raymond C. Davidson, President Davidson Corporation
SUBJ:	REDUCTION IN FORCE

You will recall that a very stringent cost-improvement program was implemented at Davidson Corporation with the expectation that the economy would recover by mid-year. Unfortunately, that has not occurred, and the economic outlook continues to be uncertain.

Therefore, it is necessary at this time to take a most difficult step and reduce the number of employees. The reduction in force will take place immediately, and affected employees at the Salt Lake City operation will be informed by their managers.

Terminated employees will be paid through September and will receive severance pay according to their years of service. We have made arrangements to provide medical and hospitalization coverage for these employees through October and will provide assistance in preparing résumés or job counseling.

Any questions concerning these actions should be directed to your immediate manager or to the Human Resources Department.

We expect market conditions to improve and hope that the remaining organization will permit us to fully meet the demands of these expected successes. This should eliminate the need for futher personnel adjustments.

TO EMPLOYEES WHO ARE BEING TERMINATED, ADVISING THEM OF THEIR BENEFITS

> TO: All Wyoming Employees
> FROM: Lyn Bassett
>   Outplacement Coordinator
> SUBJ: REDUCTION IN FORCE

In order to facilitate benefits administration and dissemination of final pay, a meeting has been arranged for Wednesday, October 6, at 8:00 A.M., on the fifth floor of the Lakeside National Bank Building, I-70 and Harlan.

Final outplacement benefits will include 30 days' pay, regular company severance pay (two weeks for each year of service—minimum, two weeks; maximum, 26 weeks), unused 19—— vacation pay, accrued 19—— vacation pay, and full medical coverage through December 8, 19——.

In addition, there will be workshops on résumé writing, interviewing, launching a job search, or going into business for oneself. These workshops and private counseling will be provided by Mr. Don Simon of STM Associates. Additional information will be available at the meeting on October 6th. If you wish these services, however, you must contact us no later than October 18, 19——.

NOTIFYING MANAGERS THAT THE COMPANY IS GOING OUT OF BUSINESS

> TO: All Managers and Supervisors
> FROM: Judy Leinweber
>   Manager Industrial Relations
> SUBJ: JEFFERSON MANUFACTURING COMPANY

It was announced today, September 17, 19——, that Jefferson Manufacturing Company will cease operations at its Boulder, Colorado, facility on December 15, 19——. This action is a result of reduced demand for lumber, primarily due to the depressed housing market. The closure will impact approximately 120 salaried and 240 hourly employees. Handling of outplacement assistance and retirement/ severance benefits is outlined below.

Salaried Employees

During the period September 17 through December 15, salaried employees will be required to report to work due to critical work demands. Only with approval from the departmental vice-president may an employee terminate prior to December 15. If an employee elects to do so without approval, or is discharged for cause, severance benefits may be forfeited. Employees who work through this 90-day period will be granted a severance equal to two weeks salary for each full year of service completed as of December 15, 19——.

Outplacement assistance will be provided. Telephones, with access to the WATS line, and typewriters will be available during this 90-day period next to Security in rooms #243 and #244, from 8:00 A.M. to 4:30 P.M. In addition, a two-day seminar, How to Conduct an Effective Job Search, will be held September 22 and 23. The emphasis will be on résumé preparation, interviewing techniques, developing a professional network, and financial planning during periods of unemployment. Employees who are interested in participating should contact James Bowman, extension 8468, no later than 2:00 P.M., Monday, September 20th.

During this 90-day notice period, salaried employees will continue to be paid on a biweekly basis and will be entitled to full receipt of life, medical, dental, and other benefit programs in which they are currently a participant, provided that required employee contributions are made. Final checks will be issued Thursday, December 14, for the pay period ending December 15, 19——. The status of each employee's benefit program will be discussed during the exit interview.

Since, at this time, no plan exists for reopening the Boulder facility, salaried employees will be terminated, not laid off. Therefore, there will be no automatic right of reemployment.

Severance and retirement benefits will be extended to all eligible salaried employees. An Early Retirement Package will be available to salaried employees who have attained 55 years of age or over and have completed a minimum of 10 years of continuous service. For salaried employees ineligible for retirement, a lump-sum severance allowance will be paid. This allowance will be based on salary and the number of full years of service completed at date of termination. Life, medical, and dental benefits will be extended beyond December 15, 19—— as reflected below:

1–5 years	30 days continuation
6–9 years	90 days continuation
10 or more years	120 days continuation

Hourly Employees

Hourly employees will be required to report to work from September 17 through December 15, 19—— in order to qualify for severance pay. Employees who work through this 90-day period will be granted severance pay equal to two weeks salary for each full year of completed service.

Hourly employees will continue to be paid on a biweekly basis and will be entitled to life, medical, and dental insurance as well as other benefit programs in which they currently participate. Final checks will be issued Thursday, December 14, for the pay period ending December 15, 19——. The status of each employee's benefit program will be discussed during the exit interview.

Recall rights will not be retained past December 15, 19——, since the facility is being closed and employees are being terminated. Should this facility reopen, employees would be given equal consideration relative to external candidates, but if rehired would not retain their prior seniority.

General

Each manager should meet with his or her respective staff immediately to announce the impending closure. Your Employee Relations representative should be present to answer any benefit-related questions and to explain scheduling of exit interviews. Employee Relations will be available to assist with outplacement and to address benefits issues. Please do not attempt to answer employee questions as they relate to the Labor Agreements or to outplacement.

Should you have any questions or wish to discuss this further, please contact the appropriate vice-president or the Employee Relations Dept. Your cooperation in meeting our production requirements and in maintaining a positive environment until final plant closure is appreciated.

Encl.

JEFFERSON MANUFACTURING COMPANY
TERMINATION CHECKLIST

Name: _____

Position: _____   Salaried: _____   Hourly: _____

Employment Date: _____

Effective Date of Termination: _____

Base Salary as of Date of Termination: _____

Full Years of Completed Service: _____   Age: _____
   (as of date of termination)   (as of date of termination)

Eligible for Bonus: _____ yes _____ no   Amount: $_____

Eligible for Early Retirement Package: _____   _____
                                      yes   no

Eligible for Severance Allowance: _____ _____
                             yes   no

(See attached calculation sheets for severance and retirement)

STATUS OF BENEFIT PLANS:

Medical Insurance: Continued through _____ provided employee contributions are made.

Life Insurance: Continued through _____ provided employee contributions are made.

Dental Insurance: Continued through _____ provided employee contributions are made.

Savings Plan: To be fully vested through date of termination, _____, regardless of service.

Employee Stock Ownership Plan (ESOP): Distribution of Company contribution and employee contribution as of date of termination, _____.

Vacation: Earned _____
Accrued _____
Taken _____
Due _____

Miscellaneous Benefits:

ITEMS TO BE COLLECTED:

Credit Cards:

American Express _____
Car Rental(s) _____
Telephone Credit _____
Other _____

Security:

Gate Pass _____
Building Access _____
Data Processing Access _____
Keys _____

Clothing/Equipment:

CLEARANCES:

Loans:

Educational Assistance _____
Payroll Advance _____
Petty Cash Advance _____
Relocation Advance _____
Other _____

This termination checklist must be completed, signed, and returned to Employee Relations prior to receipt of final check.

I acknowledge that the above benefits and their status at counseling were discussed with me.

Date: _____ Employee Signature: _____

Date: _____ Witness Signature: _____

TO MANAGERS REGARDING EEO CLAUSE
IN UNION CONTRACTS

> TO: Employee Relations Managers
>   All U.S. Locations
> FROM: P. J. Ptacek
> SUBJ: EEO CLAUSE IN UNION CONTRACTS

After review from the Legal Department and combining all the suggestions you submitted, we are providing the following wording for use in union contracts to meet our Equal Employment Opportunity obligation:

> The company and the union mutually agree that there shall be no discrimination against any employee with respect to any terms or conditions of employment because of race, color, creed, religion, sex, age, national origin, or handicap, or to Vietnam era veterans or to disabled veterans.

We believe this statement will protect our rights as well as establish union responsibility for cooperation in all areas of Equal Employment and Affirmative Action endeavors. This will provide a means of assuring that either side can demand arbitration when civil rights charges have been filed.

We also suggest that all contracts be made "sexually neutral" or that you include a brief disclaimer that explains "...whenever the masculine gender appears, it will be understood to include the feminine as well."

If I can assist you in specific negotiation situations, please call.

TO OFCCP ASKING FOR DELAY OF REVIEW
BECAUSE OF UNION CONTRACT NEGOTIATIONS

A. D. Hutchor, EOS
Office of Federal Contract Compliance Programs
Regan Office Bldg., Suite 450
Dallas, Texas 75219

Dear Ms. Hutchor:

This letter will confirm our phone conversation of January 13, 19——. Since all of our employee relations staff at the Addison, Texas facility are currently involved in negotiating a new collective bargaining agreement, we appreciate your postponing the on-site portion of the review until the new contract is approved. We anticipate that a settlement can be reached prior to the contract's April 23rd expiration date.

I will notify you as soon as the bargaining sessions end. Again, your cooperation is sincerely appreciated.

Cordially,

Patty Ptacek
Employee Relations Manager

TO VICE-PRESIDENT OF COMPANY FROM
ATTORNEY REGARDING "THE WEINGARTEN RULE"

Mr. Wesley K. Upson
Vice-President, Operations
Webcor, Inc.
4984 Washington Street
Denver, Colorado 80216

Dear Wes:

The following is a summary of the research you requested regarding an employee's right to union representation during a disciplinary interview:

A decision of the United States Supreme Court that has become known as "The Weingarten Rule" says: "An employee is entitled to have a union representative present at an investigatory interview by an employer if the employee reasonably believes that the interview might result in disciplinary action." Denial of this right may result in a make-whole remedy-reinstatement, back pay, and expunging of disciplinary records—in addition to the traditional cease-and-desist order. However, the employer can negate the above by demonstrating that its decision to discharge or discipline was not based on information obtained at the unlawful interview.

An employee is entitled to a pre-interview consultation with the person who will assist him or her at the interview and to be informed of the nature of the matter being investigated; however, the employer has no obligation to allow the employee to consult union representatives on company time before the interview if the interview date provides adequate opportunity for pre-interview consultation with union representatives on the employee's time. The employer need not postpone the interview because a union representative is unavailable for reasons for which the employer is not responsible, where the employee could have asked for another union representative. The employer is not obligated to suggest or secure alternative representation for the employee. Union representation is not required at meetings held solely to inform employees of disciplinary decisions already made.

Please call me if you have any questions.

Sincerely,

Raymond C. Delisle
Ihrig, Delisle & Associates

TO EMPLOYEES REGARDING
A UNION ORGANIZING DRIVE

Dear Employee:

You are probably aware by now that the Lincoln Power Plant employees have become the target of a union organizing drive by the Utility Workers. You can expect to be contacted by these union salespeople, and I would appreciate your taking the time to read this letter very carefully, because it talks about just what they are selling.

As is the case with most door-to-door high-pressure salespeople, the union organizer (this could include a fellow employee) is interested in getting you to sign up—to sign a card similar to the attached sample. Many of you were contacted by salespeople from the Steelworkers a couple of years ago. You didn't buy that pitch, and this one is no different. Although it may not specifically indicate that it is an application for membership in the union, you should be aware that your signature may constitute an application for membership and an authorization (should the union represent you) to withhold from your wages union dues, initiation fees, and assessments established by the union. By signing the card, you may be joining the union.

All of you know what your company's position is in this matter. Our objective is to run a union-free operation, and we sincerely feel that there isn't anything a union can do for you that we can't do better! Also, you should know that unions are covered by Union By-Laws and a Union Constitution. Before you even consider signing any card, ask the union salespeople to get you a copy of the By-Laws and the Constitution. Don't sign up until you fully understand what you are buying.

In their pitch to you, the union organizers will attempt to stir up and sell dissatisfaction. We strongly oppose what they are selling. Union agitation will not make a better place to work. When you are asked to sign that card, think about it first.

If you have any questions about this situation, please contact your supervisor or me. Thank you for your attention to this extremely important matter.

Sincerely,

Thomas C. Cleary
Labor Relations Director

TO EMPLOYEES REGARDING
A PICKET LINE AND DEMONSTRATION

   TO: All Employees
 FROM: Lane Green
     Personnel Manager
 SUBJ: BUFFALO PROJECT

There is a possibility that within the next several days a picket line or other demonstration in opposition to the Company's Buffalo Project will occur at the headquarters building.

There are currently no new developments to report concerning this project. We are continuing environmental studies and marketing efforts, and have maintained an ongoing dialogue with members of the local community to keep them informed of our activities.

For this or any other demonstration concerning any of the Company's activities, we have developed the following guidelines for employees:

- All demonstration activity should be located off company property, which is generally bounded by Long Avenue, Greenwood Drive, and 43rd Street.

- Employees should proceed to the company parking lot as usual and go directly to the building, using the main lobby entrance or the east door.
- If entry into the parking lot is blocked, do not attempt to force your way through. Proceed to an outlying parking lot area, and company vans will be dispatched to transport you to the building after the entrance has been cleared.
- Employees should avoid talking with, confronting, photographing, or otherwise alienating or inciting any demonstrator or member of the press. The Public Relations Department will make official Company news releases.

Insofar as possible, business will be carried on as usual.

TO EMPLOYEES REGARDING A UNION ELECTION

Dear Fellow Employees:

During the past few days I've had the opportunity to think about this union matter. We are frequently so busy with our day-to-day activities that we don't take the time to study a situation as thoroughly as we should. One thing I know, once a union gets into our Company it's too late to change our minds.

As I was thinking about the union I put to paper some of the costs that unionization might involve for you, and I was _shocked_. The figures are set out on the enclosed sheet so that you can see for yourself what the costs would be to you as a result of voting for union representation. Is it really worth it?

Personally, I'd like each of you to try it without a union. You can always select one in the future if you think that we have treated you unfairly.

I know it's easy to feel miffed, to believe we haven't always done the right thing, and to try to retaliate or get even with Company management. We are all working hard to meet deadlines and we have days when things don't go right. I feel that we have tried to manage fairly and evenhandedly and to provide competitive wages and benefits, but this company has made mistakes ... we are not perfect. Because of our rapid growth and pressures to meet production and shipping deadlines, our communications haven't been the best, but we hope to improve ... these things can be corrected and we are trying.

Isn't it better to face the facts honestly and discuss our mutual problems directly? We are not so big that we cannot talk to each other and work out our difficulties without the problems and costs that a union would bring.

I'm sure we can do the job together without its costing you a dime! Evaluate the costs to you of unionization. Together, we can do a better job and help each other without outside interference, and you can save your hard-earned money. LET'S TRY IT!

On election day don't take that irrevocable step of voting in a union and risking loss of income. Instead, I would appreciate your voting NO UNION ... which, in effect, is a vote for all of us. THANK YOU!

Jim Jordon
General Manager

11

Writing a Business Letter That Makes the Reader Read On

Effective writing is a result of your ability to:

• Analyze your audience and gear your letter to that person,

• Organize your material logically around a central theme,

• Eliminate unnecessary words and cumbersome phrases that obscure important ideas,

• Present a tone that makes your reader responsive to your message,

• Keep the reader's interest level high; keep the letter short,

• Avoid clichés and common writing blunders,

• Deal with problem issues and delicate subjects tactfully,

• Apply basic psychology to your letters to resolve conflict,

• Use a personal touch either at the beginning or ending of the letter,

• Go heavier on nouns and verbs, lighter on adjectives; use the active voice,

• Be very clear; don't exaggerate; distinguish opinions from facts,

• Realize that a sense of humor is refreshing, but don't be flippant if you want to be taken seriously.

Ask yourself these three questions as you start to write a letter:

1. Why are you writing the letter?
   • Explain what prompts your letter now—an answer to previous correspondence? confirm a conversation? at someone's request?
   • Stress the importance of the subject matter, if your reader is unfamiliar with it.

2. What is your letter about?
   - State your position (or problem, if position is controversial), explaining what you want your reader to do or believe as a result of reading your letter. Position usually should be stated no later than second paragraph.
   - Define special terms and give assumptions and limitations of your study.

3. How is subject to be discussed?
   - List your issues or, better still, your conclusions and recommendations, making your opening statement a summary of your letter.

Organization

One of the toughest elements of business letter-writing is deciding what order of organization you should use. There are basically three ways to organize a business letter:

Time order. In describing a series of events, you might follow a natural chronological sequence—putting the most significant facts first and leaving the least important details until last. Eliminate trivial matters.

Descriptive order. If you were to show a visitor around the plant, pointing out objects of interest in the order of their placement, you wouldn't drag the person back and forth from one corner to another. Make known your point of view from the beginning and keep to that point of view until you have completed the letter.

Expository order. In expository order, you begin with things known and proceed to things unknown. It is the order of increasing complication, and is often used in describing experiments or in technical and scientific writing.

In order to be a good business writer, you must understand the key variables in any situation. In addition, you must understand their dimensions and appreciate interrelationships so you can properly select and apply the management methods and techniques that will be effective in achieving the results you want. Just as there is no one best way to arrange a task or to manage an enterprise, there is no one best way to write a letter. A manager's effectiveness is a function of a properly interpreted situation and properly applied managerial techniques. The interpretation includes assessing the primary factors in the situation, and then selecting and applying the techniques that are appropriate to the situation as determined by the particular factors. The same process occurs in good business writing.

As you proceed to write your letter, consider the following:

Body of Letter

- Discuss issues in descending order of importance.
- Start each issue with a statement of your conclusion; then present your data supporting the conclusion.
- Present only enough data to make your conclusion clear to your key reader. Put supplementary data in an attachment.

Summing Up

- Recap your major conclusions discussed in the body of the letter.
- Restate your position.
- Give your recommendations: (a) the action program you would like the reader to carry out, or (b) the future work that you intend to do.

BEGINNINGS—THREE EASY WAYS TO START A LETTER

The hardest part of writing a letter is getting started. Here are three easy letter beginnings that will help you start any letter within seconds.

Name beginning: "John Doe suggested I write to you."

Summary beginning: Summarize significant items in order of their importance.

Question beginning: "Do your plans for the future include joining a salary survey group?"

THE POWER OF WORDS

If you want people to read your letters, pack words with power, avoid clichés, use active, appropriate words. Short words are the most powerful. Words of five syllables or more are weak. Increase your vocabulary of short, powerful words. For example: To concede a point is more stimulating than to give in. An inherent weakness works better than a built-in weakness.

In a letter to corporate executives from the personnel manager of an outlying plant explaining the tense atmosphere of a community meeting, you could say 500 people were in the auditorium to protest, or you could say 500 people *jammed* the auditorium to protest. By replacing two boring words with one active word, you instantly convey a feeling for the situation.

It's important to pick the right word for the situation. If a situation is risky, it's probably less serious than if it's a perilous undertaking. The degree of severity should dictate the words you use to portray a specific situation.

MANAGER'S TIPS ON PARAGRAPHS, SENTENCES, EVALUATION

Paragraphs

- Limit each paragraph to one topic.
- Begin each paragraph with a topic sentence.
- Limit your paragraphs to four to five sentences, or about 1 to 1½ inches, single spaced.

Sentences

- Limit sentences to a maximum of two ideas, or two verbs.
- Check every sentence over three lines, counting the number of verbs it contains.
- Omit unnecessary words, checking each word to see whether it can be left out, or if one or two words can be used instead of three or more.
- Use only words you would use in conversation with your key reader.
- Keep the verb at the beginning of the sentence.

Evaluate

- Organization
- Completeness
- Clearness
- Accuracy
- Conciseness
- Courtesy
- Empathy
- Interest
- Style, tone

252 WORDS YOU CAN USE TO PACK YOUR WRITING WITH POWER

Being frugal with the number of words used gives your writing more power. The word "arguably" seems difficult and dense, but other ways of saying the same thing require more words. "It can be argued that," "according to some people." The one word, arguably, strengthens the sentence.

Power words, used in the right place, are critical to your writing success. Here are 252 words you can use to pack your business letters with power.

initial claims	*simulated* moon environment
based on the *assumption*	a *raucous* voice
an *ironical* situation	a *garrulous* person
speaking *simultaneously*	*grass roots* nature
tentative plans	a *vehement* response
an *aggressive* labor policy	*stereotyped* in his views
compensated for the loss	*sporadic* attempts
a *poignant* story	*basic* principles
methods of *retaliation*	of *nondescript* appearance
inherent weaknesses	an *apathetic* outlook
an *enervating* task	an *audacious* child
a *perfunctory* remark	a person of *affluence*
an *obsequious* manner	the political *incumbent*
an *unsullied* reputation	unflinching *fortitude*

a *resplendent* array

an *inveterate* gambler

adroit movements

conversational *gambits*

vociferous in his speech

unilateral agreements

averse to change

peremptory dismissal

a *predilection* for the truth

a justifiable *tenet*

a *trite* expression

a *perceptible* change

derelict in his duty

an object of *derision*

latent possibilities

a *pertinent* reply

succinct remarks

decadent civilization

a striking *analogy*

a *diffident* person

agility of movement

a *motley* array

to *rescind* a motion

a *voracious* reader

a feeling of *empathy*

disparaging comments

a well-chosen *excerpt*

the *resonance* of his voice

a *condescending* attitude

a *rhetorical* question

tantamount to victory

unlikely to *acquiesce*

a *sagacious* answer

viewed with *skepticism*

to *concede* a point

in *unprecedented* numbers

political *aspirations*

germane to the question

the *prosaic* style

urbane in manner

defamation of character

an *ostentatious* display

frenetic outbursts

a *syndicated* column

unscrupulous attacks

an *insinuating* remark

a *perennial* favorite

a *persistent* rumor

epicurean tastes

expunged from his mind

in danger of *atrophy*

astronomical proportions

sanguine disposition

an *onerous* task

a question of *semantics*

a *conciliatory* attitude

a strange *anomaly*

gamut of emotions

a *feasible* plan

an *insidious* problem

a land of *incredible* beauty

to *ambush* them

a *posthumous* award

an *innocuous* remark

accused of *collusion*

a *furtive* glance

gregarious in his habits

dogmatic statements

fallacious statements

a *facile* style of writing

a recognized *prerogative*

an *untenable* position

clichés in speech

intimidating remarks

a *vicarious* experience

a *blatant* voice

a *verbose* individual

ambiguous statements

apropos questions

irrelevant arguments

an *incongruous* situation

a *fatuous* character

hackneyed phrases

a *droll* sense of humor

a *feasible* plan

a *sinister* expression

an *ambulatory* patient

to *surmount* all difficulties

a *grueling* experience

a *perilous* undertaking

no other *alternative*

to *retrieve* a loss

greater than his *predecessor*

behaving like a *renegade*

facing *annihilation*

rising *antagonism*

a *fervid* plea
a *caustic* answer
devoted to a *fetish*
a *presumptuous* manner
penurious habits
a *tranquilizing* effect
a *baleful* look
an *optimistic* outlook
a *premonition* of danger
attempts to *contrive*
mutually acceptable
illusions of power
an *anthology* of poetry
a *phenomenal* success
a *sinister* expression
adept in dealing with others
in the process of *litigation*
a *penchant* for writing
a *glib* speaker
obsolete words
a *proxy* vote
chronic ailments
a noticeable *grimace*
a *macabre* display
a *candid* opinion
a *vapid* speech
a *strident* voice
fortuitous circumstances
an attack of *lethargy*
a *concerted* course of action
a feeling of *apathy*
turbulent times
to *minimize* your efforts
a plan of *infiltration*
a *cursory* analysis
a *sacrilegious* remark
susceptible to infection
to *misconstrue* a statement
to *indict* a person
an *indigent* individual
a *quixotic* temperament
dexterous movements
detecting an *innuendo*
a *novice* in acting
mediocre talents
potentially dangerous
to *stagnate* indefinitely
devoutly dedicated

chronic ailments
an *altruistic* nature
a *cogent* argument
ready to *capitulate*
salutary effects
a *symbolic* dance
to *supplement* his income
a *jaundiced* view
the habits of a *scavenger*
a feeling of *nostalgia*
indomitable spirit
a well-known *benefactor*
predestined to fail
an *apparent* mistake
a *discrepancy* in views
an unforgettable *holocaust*
a *scintillating* personality
an *orthodox* procedure
an *auspicious* occasion
a *beguiling* smile
a *stipulated* amount
a *lucrative* position
a *maudlin* display
a *reticent* nature
a *sinister* expression
an *ebbing* interest
a *provocative* statement
manifestly unfair
an *obstacle* course
an *arbitrary* ruling
to *jeopardize* the future
disruption of the economy
his personal *prestige*
less *obvious* advantage
accept the *status quo*
inclined to *digress*
sibilant sounds
a recent *proselyte*
a *benign* smile
mixed *metaphors*
unverified charges
coherent statements
a *voluble* spokesman
an *infirm* hand
impaired vision
cumulative effects
rampant rumors
a *precarious* undertaking

obsessed with the idea	a *decrepit* appearance
a part of the *clique*	an enjoyable *respite*
the *arrogance* of a dictator	*facetious* remarks
a *dynamic* personality	*hypothetical* circumstances
to *liquidate* his holdings	an *amenable* person
dire predictions	*chronic* ailments
feigning surprise	a *noncommittal* answer
a study of *logistics*	an *insatiable* desire
a familiar *idiom*	a *convivial* group
notorious for his deeds	an occasion of *levity*
a *climactic* year	*vacillating* in his opinions
an *eminent* attorney	*oblivious* of the consequences
a *scrutinizing* look	*obtuse* in his thinking
proponents of foreign aid	to *forfeit* the game
of *titanic* strength	a *gruesome* sight
diversified interests	motor *mayhem*

WRITING WITHOUT BIAS

Even though most organizations have taken giant steps toward eliminating racial and sexual discrimination on the job, and carefully screen racism and sexism from ads, internal communications are frequently overlooked and bias in writing is quite common.

Do these situations sound familiar?

- The CEO of a large organization writes a congratulatory letter to a black manager who has just won a prestigious award. The letter closes with this statement: "You are a credit to our organization, and to your people."
  The CEO should have ended the letter after saying, "You are a credit to our organization."

- A woman executive has just completed a major market research project that enabled her company to obtain a multi-million-dollar contract. Her boss outlined the research project that led to the contract in a letter to the CEO by saying, "Miss Jones is one of the best girls on my staff."

Improper punctuation can also imply bias and significantly change the meaning of your message.

"This group is also weighted more toward females, who are secondary earners for the family..."

or

"This group is also weighted more toward females who are secondary earners for the family..."

Without the comma, the meaning is entirely different.

Most bias in writing is unconscious, but that doesn't make it easier to handle if you are the subject, and the recipient, of such a letter.

Communications Guidelines for Avoiding Bias

The most important element in avoiding bias in your letters is awareness.

The second most important item is to add some alternative words and phrases to your vocabulary.

Here are some examples:

- Older people don't like to be referred to as "elderly," "golden ager," and so forth. They prefer "senior citizen" or "older person."

- "Minority" accurately identifies people when they are in a minority, but a more sensitive phrase is "member of a minority group," or "minority group member."

- Women accept the use of "person," but person is a thinly disguised alternative for "women." A female can be a "chairperson," but the term "leader" works as well.

- "Human resources" includes everyone; "manpower" does not.

- If you are writing a letter and are not positive whether the person is a man or a woman, check before you send the letter even if you have to call the company first.

  When I receive a letter addressed to "Mr. Cook," it goes into the round file.

  If you can't check and aren't sure of the sex of the addressee, don't use a salutation—or use something like "Dear Colleague."

- People with disabilities generally prefer to be described as disabled rather than handicapped.

Remember to communicate only what is relevant. Bias often lies behind statements intended to emphasize an open-minded attitude. We've all heard the "some of my best friends" disclaimer.

Avoid clichés that create offensive generalities and stereotypes: "Isn't that just like a woman?" the "passionate Spaniard," and so on.

The most common forms of bias are sexist expressions. They are used so much that they are difficult to eliminate, but the subtle consequences are tremendous, especially in letter writing.

Sexist Expressions and Non-Sexist Alternatives

Manmade:	Hand-made, synthetic
Manpower:	Human resources, workers, personnel, work force
Man-hours:	Staff time, working hours
Gentleman's agreement:	Verbal contract

Avoid masculine gender pronouns.

Rewrite sentences by changing singular pronouns to plural.

Sexist and Non-Sexist Terms

Chairman:	Chairperson, the chair
Businessman:	Business person, executive, manager
Spokesman:	Spokesperson, representative, official

Salesman:	Sales clerk, sales representative, salesperson
Workman:	Worker, laborer
Foreman:	Supervisor, boss
Layman:	Layperson, amateur
Repairman:	Plumber, electrician, etc.
Cameraman:	Photographer, camera operator
Layout man:	Layout artist
Lineman:	Installer
Watchman:	Watch, security person, guard
Pressman:	Press operator
Longshoreman:	Dock worker, stevedore

Sexist and Non-Sexist Verbs

Man the phones, pumps:	Handle the phones, operate the pumps
Man the exhibit, show, sales floor:	Staff the exhibit, run the show, supervise the sales floor
Man the control center, operating room:	Staff the control center, cover the operating room

More Tips

Avoid "girl," "gal," and "lady" when talking about an adult woman.

Break the habit of listing men first.

Resist the temptation to preface the title "doctor," "lawyer," "judge," and so forth, with "woman" when referring to professional women.

Drop the diminutive suffixes "-ess," "-ette," and "-trix" (sculptress, usherette, aviatrix).

Use "Ms." when addressing women, especially in business.

The International Association of Business Communicators has published an excellent guide entitled *Without Bias: A Guidebook for Nondiscriminatory Communication*. The book may be obtained from the IABC, 870 Market Street, San Francisco, CA 94102 at $4.00 per copy.

Important Writing Tips

- Put yourself in the reader's shoes. Show empathy. Eliminate bias.
- Write like you talk.
- Use contractions.
- Use first person.
- *Think* about what you want to say before you write.
- Be interesting.
- Increase your vocabulary to include a greater variety of power words.
- Write with class. Eliminate errors.

Checklist for Revising and Editing Your Business Letters

Revising a letter calls for systematically reading the letter several times, checking each time for a different purpose. Check the letter's content and organization, clarity of expression, and mechanics of style and form, adaptation to the reader, and general readability. The following questions provide a checklist for revising your letters.

To check contents:

1. Have the purpose and objectives been attained?
2. Is the letter accurate and complete?
   - Background material?
   - Numerical data?
   - Supporting evidence?
   - Explanations?
   - Scope?
   - Examples?
   - Facts and figures?
3. Do major and minor issues stand out in proper perspective?
4. Is there a logical development and flow of ideas?
5. Are the conclusions sound, logical, definite, and clear?
6. Are the recommendations an outgrowth of the conclusions, and are they workable?

To check organization:

1. Does the overall organization present the total picture?
2. Are all the parts related?
3. Is there a logical sequence of topics and ideas?
4. Is there general coherence and unity throughout the letter?
5. Have appropriate transitions been made?

To check for clearness of expression:

1. Are specific facts and details given?
2. Are short sentences predominant?
3. Is there an average sentence length of 17 to 22 words per sentence?
4. Are sentences varied according to structure, length, and type?
5. Are the words used concrete, familiar, precise, and simple?

To check the mechanics of style and form:

1. Is correct usage followed in spelling, punctuation, and grammar?
2. Does the report conform to a standard form for its type—letter, memorandum, short form, or long form?

3. Are correct typing details of form, margins, spacing, subject headings, and so on, followed? Does the letter *look* good?

4. Is there consistency of form?

To check readability and adaptation:

1. Has the appropriate level of readability been maintained?

2. Has the proper tone been maintained?

3. Has the reader been told enough to understand the report?

4. Has the material been adapted to the reader's knowledge and experience?

5. Has interest been gained through the vocabulary, layout, and approach to the subject?

6. Has the reader's need been recognized?

The extent to which this checklist is used will depend on the writer's experience and abilities and the time available for revisions. Short letters don't need to be revised through such a long process, but letters that go to employees setting out specific benefits, compensation, and timing of a layoff, for example, should be revised and edited through a set procedure to ensure accuracy. The letter might later be construed as a formal contract.

COMMON USAGE MISTAKES TO AVOID

There is confusion over the subtleties and fine points of word usage. Some people fuss over simple word interchanges, like the words *bring* or *take*, and the argument over which of these words is the right one to use in a specific situation is probably a waste of time; but if you value precision and want your letters to make a favorable impression on the sophisticated reader, you should at least be aware of the distinctions even if you wish to disregard some of them.

Here are a few of the more obvious word interchanges:

accept – except. Accept, a verb; it means to take, to receive. Except, a verb, means to exclude, to exempt. Except, a preposition, means other than, excluding. Never use *but* for *except*.

adverse – averse. Adverse means unfavorable. Averse means unwilling.

advice – advise. Advice is a noun, meaning to give advice. Advise is a verb; you advise someone.

affect – effect. Affect, a verb, means to move emotionally. Effect, a verb, means to influence; effect, a noun, is a result or outcome.

all together – altogether. All together means in one group; altogether means completely, thoroughly.

allusion – illusion. An allusion is a reference; an illusion is a deceptive appearance.

a lot. Is always written as two words—never one word.

complement – compliment. Complement is something that balances or enhances. Compliment expresses approval or praise.

discreet – discrete. Discreet means tactful or careful of your words and actions. Discrete means separate and unrelated.

elicit – illicit. Elicit means to draw out, as a response. Illicit means illegal or unlawful.

eminent – imminent. Eminent means noteworthy. Imminent means impending, likely to happen any minute.

farther – further. Farther refers to distance; further refers to degree or to greater extent.

if – whether. If suggests a condition in which there are no alternatives. Whether indicates alternatives. Do not use "whether or not" where merely "whether" would suffice.

principal – principle. Principal is the main factor. Principle refers to a standard of judgment or conduct.

These are only a few of the more prominent word interchanges that give us problems in everyday letter writing. There are many more. The professional business writer knows the correct word to use.

Use Simplifying Phrases

Don't Use	*Do Use*
a great number of times	often
in excess of	more
in the neighborhood of	about
until such time	until, when
a greater number of	more
in view of the fact that	considering
make application to	apply
a little less than	almost
at a later date	later
a majority of	most
at all times	always
for the purpose of	for, to
a small number of	few
at an early date	soon
despite the fact that	although
for the reason that	because
a large number of	many
for this reason	so
is of the opinion that	believes

Don't Use	Do Use
more and more	increasingly
a period of several weeks	several weeks
at that time	then
is representative of	typifies
a sufficient number	enough
at the present time	now
due to the fact that	because
from time to time	occasionally
with regard to	about, regarding

TROUBLESHOOTING GUIDE TO REDUNDANCIES, INTENSIFIERS, AND DEAD WOOD

By eliminating marathon sentences, deadwood in phrasing, unnecessary intensifiers, and redundant words, you will increase the readability of your letters. Here are a few of the most common elements of poor business writing that you can easily spot and eliminate:

- Phrases that are too long. Change "in order to" to "to."

- Marathon sentences and paragraphs. Sentences should contain no more than 15 to 17 words; paragraphs no more than four or five sentences.

- Intensifiers. Words such as "very," "great deal," "many," should be eliminated.

- Redundancies. "As a general rule," or "a serious crisis" are two common redundancies.

- Pretense. Watch for words of three syllables or more. Switch "facilitate" to "aid," "expedite" to "speed," and "available" to "ready." Most business people are not impressed by pretense in writing.

- Dead wood. Eliminate the trite phrases, such as: "In response to your letter of January 13, 19——," "please be advised that," "you will be interested to hear."

- Usage. Check to make sure you've used the correct word. If you've used "affect" when you should have used "effect," one signal to readers is that you don't understand appropriate English usage. It could make a difference in their opinion of your professionalism.

CLICHÉ SURVIVAL KIT

Anyone who is called upon to write a significant number of letters on a regular basis needs a cliché "survival kit."

An executive who wants to survive will "pull out all stops" to "nail down all the facts" before writing a letter that "hits the nail on the head." In addition, "a word of caution is in order" so you won't "upset any applecarts" as you communicate through business letters.

Most business people don't like writing that is muddled with clichés, but if you "take the bull by the horns," even though "the chips are down," and "put your shoulder to the wheel" and "your nose to the grindstone," your writing can improve and you might even get a "clean bill of health."

Get the message?

WORD PROCESSING AND THE ELECTRONIC OFFICE

Offices today provide data and text communication options in interactive or batch communications through phone lines tied directly to a mainframe computer, enabling the manipulation of data using standard word processing functions.

Marilyn Showers, CPS, owner of Golden Hill Secretarial, Inc., Lakewood, Colorado, says that offices are changing rapidly. No longer can a company operate efficiently with a typewriter as its only source of document generation, a mail room as its only source of document receipt, and file drawers as its only source of memory.

Now a word processor is able to key in data and/or text and have it picked up almost instantly on the screen of another machine by telecommunicating it over phone lines from one station to another, whether in the same building, across town, or in another state. And that text or data remains on diskette until it is no longer needed, at which time it may be deleted. No longer must you go through drawer after drawer of files, scanning folder after folder of papers, to decide whether certain information needs to be retained.

With a word processor, too, all documents may be set up in a special format, lending consistency and good looks to work done. The margins, spacing, line requirements, right-margin justification, and page numbering for a particular company's letterhead or reports can be put into the machine as defaults so that all documents generated are consistently the same. A letter-perfect result each time (no erasures or correction tape), can be assured through proper formatting and a spell/hyphenate checking feature on most word processors.

It is now well known just how simple it is to edit existing data or text within a word processor. If desired, one can duplicate an entire report, to retain it in its original form, and then proceed to "cut and paste" via the keyboard to make it an entirely new document—yet with the same margins and line format. At the same time that editing on one document is taking place, the machine is capable of printing out other items or merging a mailing list with a "shell" letter for an unlimited number of personalized repetitive letters.

With voice-synthesized word processors and OCR (optical character recognition) machines, it is becoming more apparent that keyboarding, per se, will not be the only method of inputting text or data.

For some businesses, it is more important to have a signed document quickly than a printout of that document, unsigned, from a word processor. For occasions such as this, the facsimile transceiver can be put to good use—allowing the recipient to have an exact copy of a signed document within two to four minutes.

A TWX/Telex machine is another way in which messages can be handled expeditiously. It allows one to send or receive a telegram, cablegram, or mailgram. As soon as the message is formatted by the sender and the proper number dialed or keyed in, it is received by the addressee.

Another helpful tool during these fast-paced times is a dictating machine, accessed via any touch-tone phone, which gives a dictating party 90 minutes of time per tape cassette.

Teleconferencing makes it possible for people in various parts of the world to hold meetings without the need for travel, but with the "personal" touch of seeing each other.

Yes, without a doubt we are deeply into the age of communication and telecommunication. The electronic office is here, and each year it becomes more sophisticated and efficient.

AND IN CONCLUSION

Writing effective business correspondence is a matter of keeping the principles in mind and brushing up on the techniques. The following checklist should aid you in both efforts. Review it occasionally, particularly when the correspondence involved may have implications beyond the acts of writing it and reading it. Business correspondence is an extension of the writer and the firm the writer represents. Make certain the impression conveyed is a positive one.

CHECKLIST FOR ORGANIZING AND WRITING BUSINESS LETTERS

- ☐ Organize your thoughts first and establish your purpose in writing the letter.
- ☐ Identify your audience. What will your reader be looking for? Visualize the reader ... age, position, education, interests.
- ☐ Get all the facts. If you are answering a letter, have it handy. Complete any research that's needed before you start to write.
- ☐ Letters should have personality. Set a positive tone, be warm and considerate, use humor.

☐ Get to the point in the first paragraph. Busy people don't like to hunt for the message. Ask the reader to take any action that is necessary in the last paragraph.

☐ Keep the letter short—one page if possible. Short sentences are the most effective.

☐ Be specific. Give numbers, amounts, places. Get all the facts right up front.

☐ Handle bad news gently. Ease into it. Use considerate phrases: "Thank you for," "We're sorry that." Putting bad news first is unprofessional and unkind.

☐ If the letter is a tough one to write, or is written in anger or disappointment, sleep on it. Read it the next day and revise as necessary.

☐ Be sure you know the person you are writing to. Use the correct name, title, and gender. Eliminate bias from your writing.

☐ Don't put on airs by using big words. Pretense only impresses the pretender. The reader is bored and turned off. Power words are short.

☐ Distinguish opinions from fact; don't exaggerate and don't lie. Your reader will spot emotional or untruthful ploys, and your credibility will be lost.

☐ Use a simple, honest close. If the letter is a difficult one, like the turndown of a job, don't sign it "Cordially." Wish the applicant success in the search for a job and sign it "Sincerely."

☐ Edit your letters. Eliminate overloaded sentences and unnecessary words. Eliminate qualifiers such as "apparently," "hopefully," "undoubtedly." They weaken the message.

☐ When you've finished your letter, read it over. Does it convey the message you intended in an interesting, succinct manner?

☐ Keep a file of sample letters—the ones you thought achieved their purposes.

J